I0007414

Golang programming:

Streamline Your Code and Scale Your Applications
with the Power of Go: A Practical Guide to Writing
Clean, Efficient, and Concurrent Programs

Matthew D.Passmore

All rights reserved. No part of this publication may be
reproduced, distributed, or transmitted in any form or by
any means, including photocopying, recording, or other
electronic or mechanical methods, without the prior written
permission of the publisher, except in the case of brief
quotations embodied in critical reviews and certain other
noncommercial uses permitted by copyright law.

Copyright © Matthew D.Passmore
(2025)

Table of Content"

Chapter 6: Optimizing Performance

6.1 Understanding Go's Runtime

6.2 Memory Optimization and Garbage Collection

6.3 Reducing Latency and Improving Throughput

6.4 Using pprof for Performance Analysis

Part III: Concurrency and Scalability

.

Chapter 7: Concurrency in Go

7.1 Goroutines: Lightweight Threads

7.2 Channels: Communicating Between Goroutines

7.3 Select Statements and Patterns

7.4 Synchronization with sync Package

Chapter 8: Advanced Concurrency Patterns

8.1 Worker Pools

8.2 Fan-In and Fan-Out Patterns

8.3 Context Package for Cancellation and Timeouts

8.4 Avoiding Common Concurrency Pitfalls

Chapter 9: Building Scalable Applications

Part I: Getting Started with Go

Chapter 1
Introduction to Go

Go, often referred to as Golang, is an open-source programming language developed by Google in 2007 and officially released in 2009. Designed by Robert Griesemer, Rob Pike, and Ken Thompson, Go was created to address the shortcomings of other languages in terms of simplicity, efficiency, and scalability for modern software development.

Why Go?

Simplicity: Go's syntax is clean and minimalistic, making it easy to learn and read. It avoids unnecessary complexity, such as inheritance and generics (until Go 1.18), which helps developers focus on solving problems rather than navigating language intricacies.

Performance: Go is a compiled language, producing fast and efficient binaries. Its performance is comparable to low-level languages like C and C++, making it ideal for high-performance applications.

Concurrency: Go has built-in support for concurrency through goroutines and channels, enabling developers to write highly scalable and concurrent programs with ease.

Cross-Platform: Go supports cross-compilation, allowing developers to build applications for multiple platforms (Windows, Linux, macOS, etc.) from a single codebase.

Strong Ecosystem: Go comes with a rich standard library and a growing ecosystem of third-party tools and frameworks, making it suitable for a wide range of applications, from web development to cloud-native systems.

Key Features

Garbage Collection: Automatic memory management reduces the risk of memory leaks.

Static Typing: Ensures type safety and catches errors at compile time.

Fast Compilation: Go's compiler is incredibly fast, enabling quick iteration during development.

Built-in Testing: The testing package makes it easy to write and run unit tests and benchmarks.

Use Cases
Go is widely used in:

Cloud and Network Services: Docker, Kubernetes, and Terraform are built with Go.

Web Development: High-performance APIs and backend services.

DevOps Tools: Automation, monitoring, and infrastructure management.

Microservices: Scalable and maintainable distributed systems.

In summary, Go is a modern, efficient, and developer-friendly language that combines the best of both worlds: the performance of low-level languages and the simplicity of high-level languages. Its focus on concurrency and scalability makes it an excellent choice for building robust, high-performance applications in today's fast-paced tech landscape.

1.1 What is Go?

Go, commonly referred to as Golang, is an open-source, statically typed, compiled programming language designed for simplicity, efficiency, and scalability. It was created by Google in 2007 by Robert Griesemer, Rob Pike, and Ken Thompson, with the goal of addressing the challenges faced by developers when building large-scale, high-performance software systems. Go was officially released to the public in 2009 and has since gained widespread adoption in the tech industry.

Key Characteristics of Go

Simplicity:

Go was designed with a minimalistic and clean syntax, making it easy to learn and use. It avoids complex features like inheritance and generics (until Go 1.18), which reduces the cognitive load on developers and encourages writing clear, maintainable code.

Performance:

As a compiled language, Go produces highly optimized machine code, resulting in fast execution speeds comparable to low-level languages like C and C++. This makes it ideal for performance-critical applications.

Concurrency:

Go has built-in support for concurrency through goroutines (lightweight threads) and channels (for communication between goroutines). This makes it easy to write programs that can handle thousands of concurrent tasks efficiently, a key requirement for modern distributed systems.

Garbage Collection:

Go includes automatic memory management, which helps prevent memory leaks and reduces the burden of manual memory allocation and deallocation.

Static Typing:

Go is statically typed, meaning type checking is done at compile time. This ensures type safety and helps catch errors early in the development process.

Cross-Platform:

Go supports cross-compilation, allowing developers to build applications for multiple operating systems (Windows, Linux, macOS, etc.) from a single codebase.

Rich Standard Library:

Go comes with a comprehensive standard library that includes packages for networking, file handling, cryptography, and more. This reduces the need for third-party dependencies and simplifies development.

Fast Compilation:

Go's compiler is incredibly fast, enabling quick iteration and reducing development time.

Why Was Go Created?

Go was developed to address the shortcomings of existing programming languages in the context of modern software development. At Google, engineers faced challenges with large-scale systems, including:

Slow build times with languages like C++ and Java.

Complexity in managing dependencies and concurrency.

Lack of a language that balanced performance, simplicity, and productivity.

Go was designed to solve these problems by providing a language that is:

Easy to learn and use.

Efficient and fast.

Scalable and concurrent.

Suitable for modern cloud and networked environments.

Use Cases for Go

Go is widely used in a variety of domains, including:

Cloud and Network Services: Tools like Docker, Kubernetes, and Terraform are built with Go.

Web Development: Go is used to build high-performance APIs, web servers, and backend services.

DevOps and Automation: Go is popular for writing tools for infrastructure management, monitoring, and automation.

Microservices: Go's simplicity and concurrency features make it a great choice for building scalable microservices architectures.

Command-Line Tools: Go's fast compilation and small binary sizes make it ideal for creating efficient CLI tools.

Conclusion

Go is a modern programming language that combines the performance of low-level languages with the simplicity and productivity of high-level languages. Its focus on concurrency, scalability, and ease of use has made it a popular choice for building robust, high-performance applications in areas like cloud computing, web development, and DevOps. Whether you're a beginner or an experienced developer, Go offers a powerful and efficient toolset for tackling today's software challenges.

1.2 Why Choose Go for Modern Development?

Go, also known as Golang, was created by Google to address challenges in modern software development, particularly around performance, scalability, and simplicity. Since its release in 2009, Go has gained widespread adoption across industries, from cloud computing and web development to distributed systems and microservices. Here's why Go stands out as an excellent choice for modern development:

1. Simplicity and Readability

Go was designed to be simple, with a clean and minimalistic syntax. It avoids unnecessary complexity, making it easier to read and maintain code. Unlike languages that rely heavily on feature-rich libraries and frameworks, Go focuses on built-in functionalities, reducing the need for external dependencies.

2. Efficient Concurrency Model

Modern applications often require handling multiple tasks simultaneously, whether it's processing requests in a web server or managing background tasks. Go's built-in concurrency features, including goroutines and channels, make it easy to write highly concurrent programs without the complexity of traditional threading models.

3. High Performance with a Compiled Language

Go is a statically typed, compiled language, which means it is significantly faster than interpreted languages like Python or JavaScript. Its lightweight runtime and efficient memory management ensure that applications perform well even under high workloads.

4. Garbage Collection and Memory Safety

Go includes an optimized garbage collector that ensures efficient memory management with minimal impact on performance. Unlike languages that require manual memory management (such as C or C++), Go's automatic garbage collection reduces the risk of memory leaks and segmentation faults.

5. Strong Standard Library

Go's standard library is extensive, providing built-in support for networking, file handling, encryption, JSON processing, and more. This reduces the reliance on third-party libraries and ensures consistency and security across projects.

6. Cross-Platform and Cloud-Native

Go's ability to compile into a single binary without external dependencies makes it ideal for cloud-native development and microservices. It integrates well with Docker, Kubernetes, and cloud platforms like AWS, Google Cloud, and Azure.

7. Built-in Tooling for Productivity

Go comes with a set of built-in tools, such as:

go fmt for automatic code formatting
go test for testing

go build for compiling code

go vet for static analysis

These tools streamline development and help maintain high code quality.

8. Growing Ecosystem and Community

Go has a strong, active community and is backed by major companies like Google, Uber, Dropbox, and Netflix. The ecosystem continues to grow with powerful frameworks, libraries, and tools that make development faster and more efficient.

Conclusion

Go's simplicity, concurrency model, high performance, and cloud-native capabilities make it a top choice for modern software development. Whether you're building microservices, APIs, web applications, or distributed systems, Go provides a reliable and efficient foundation.

1.3 Key Features of Go: Simplicity, Concurrency, and Performance

Go is celebrated for its elegant simplicity, robust concurrency model, and high performance. These key features make it a powerful tool for building modern, scalable, and efficient applications. Let's explore each of these aspects in detail:

1. Simplicity

Clean and Readable Syntax:

Go was designed with simplicity in mind. Its syntax is minimalistic and clear, reducing the cognitive load for developers. This simplicity makes the language easier to learn and the code more maintainable. Unlike some other languages burdened with excessive keywords or overly complex constructs, Go encourages writing straightforward and idiomatic code.

Minimalistic Language Design:

The language intentionally avoids features that can lead to overly complicated designs, such as inheritance hierarchies and generics (though generics were introduced later, they are implemented in a way that preserves the language's overall simplicity). This design philosophy means developers can focus more on solving problems rather than wrestling with the language itself.

Powerful Standard Library:

Go comes with an extensive standard library that covers a wide range of functionalities—from networking and file I/O to data manipulation and encryption. This built-in support reduces the need for external dependencies and encourages best practices through standardized approaches.

2. Concurrency

Goroutines – Lightweight Threads:
One of Go's standout features is its concurrency model built around goroutines. Goroutines are functions that can run concurrently with other functions. They are extremely lightweight compared to traditional threads, allowing developers to run thousands of them concurrently without a significant performance penalty. This is particularly

advantageous in applications like web servers and microservices, where handling many simultaneous tasks is essential.

Channels for Communication:

Channels in Go provide a safe and structured way for goroutines to communicate and synchronize their work. By using channels, developers can pass data between concurrent routines without resorting to complex locking mechanisms. This approach helps avoid common pitfalls associated with multi-threading, such as race conditions and deadlocks.

Select Statement:

The select statement enhances concurrency by allowing a goroutine to wait on multiple communication operations. This makes it easier to build complex, responsive systems that can handle multiple streams of data and events simultaneously.

Built-in Synchronization Tools:

Beyond goroutines and channels, Go's standard library includes the sync package, which offers primitives like mutexes and wait groups. These tools provide additional support for synchronizing concurrent operations when necessary, offering developers flexibility without sacrificing the language's simplicity.

3. Performance
Compiled Language Efficiency:

Go is a compiled language, meaning the source code is transformed directly into machine code. This compilation process results in high-performance executables that run efficiently on the target hardware. The static type system further contributes to performance by enabling the compiler to optimize the code during compilation.

Efficient Memory Management:

Go features an efficient garbage collector that automates memory management. This garbage collector is designed to work seamlessly with the language's concurrency model, ensuring that memory is managed effectively without imposing significant overhead. This balance of automation and efficiency helps developers avoid common memory management errors while still achieving excellent performance.

Optimized for Modern Hardware:

The language and its runtime are optimized to take advantage of modern multicore processors. By making concurrency a first-class citizen and providing tools to harness parallelism, Go allows applications to scale well with increasing hardware capabilities. This makes it particularly suitable for developing high-throughput and low-latency applications.

Tooling and Profiling Support:

Go's ecosystem includes robust tools for performance analysis and optimization, such as pprof for profiling CPU and memory usage. These tools empower developers to identify and address performance bottlenecks effectively, ensuring that applications can run at peak efficiency in production environments.

Conclusion

Go's focus on simplicity, concurrency, and performance makes it an ideal choice for modern development. Its clean syntax and minimalistic design lower the barrier to entry and enhance maintainability, while its powerful concurrency model enables developers to build highly scalable systems. Coupled with the efficiency of a compiled language and strong support for performance optimization, Go provides a comprehensive environment for creating robust, high-performance applications in today's fast-paced, resource-intensive computing landscape.

1.4 Setting Up Your Go Development Environment

Setting up your Go development environment is a straightforward process that lays the foundation for efficient coding and seamless project management. Here's a step-by-step guide to help you get started:

1. Installing Go

Download the Installer:

Visit the official Go website and download the installer appropriate for your operating system (Windows, macOS, or Linux). The website provides clear instructions and checksums to verify the integrity of your download.

Run the Installer:

Once downloaded, run the installer and follow the on-screen instructions. The installation process will typically set up the Go runtime, compiler, and essential tools on your system.

Alternative Methods:

For Linux users or those preferring command-line tools, you can use package managers like apt, yum, or brew (for macOS) to install Go. For example, on macOS with Homebrew, you might run:

```bash
Copy code
brew install go
```

2. Verifying the Installation

After installing, open your terminal or command prompt and run:

```bash
Copy code
go version
```

This command should display the installed Go version, confirming that your installation was successful.

3. Configuring Your Workspace

GOPATH and Workspace Structure:

Go uses a workspace structure to organize your code, typically defined by the GOPATH environment variable. By default, this might be set to a directory like ~/go on Unix-like systems or %USERPROFILE%\go on Windows. Inside your workspace, you'll find three key directories:

src: Where your Go source files reside.
pkg: Where package objects are stored.
bin: Where executable binaries are compiled.
You can set the GOPATH variable in your shell profile if you decide to use a custom workspace location:

```bash
Copy code
export GOPATH=$HOME/mygo
```

Module Support:

With the introduction of Go modules (enabled by default in Go 1.16 and later), you no longer need to strictly adhere to the traditional GOPATH structure. You can initialize a module in any directory using:

```bash
Copy code
go mod init my-module-name
```

Modules simplify dependency management and make your project more portable.

4. Choosing an Integrated Development Environment (IDE) or Editor

Popular IDEs and Editors:

Visual Studio Code (VS Code):
With the Go extension, VS Code offers features like code completion, linting, debugging, and integrated terminal support.

GoLand:

A powerful IDE by JetBrains, tailored specifically for Go development, offering intelligent code assistance, refactoring, and debugging tools.

Vim/Neovim:

With plugins such as vim-go, these editors can provide robust Go support if you prefer a modal editing experience.

Setting Up Your Editor:

Install the Go extension or plugin for your chosen editor. These tools often provide features like automatic code formatting (using go fmt), inline documentation, and error detection, which are invaluable during development.

5. Go Tools and Extensions

Formatting and Linting:

go fmt: Automatically formats your code to adhere to standard Go conventions.
golint: Provides style and correctness suggestions.

Testing and Benchmarking:

go test: Integrated tool for running unit tests.
go bench: Used for running benchmarks to evaluate performance.

Version Control Integration:

Set up Git (or your preferred version control system) to manage your project's source code. Most editors and IDEs offer seamless Git integration, making it easier to track changes and collaborate with others.

Chapter 2
Go Basics

The foundation of Go programming is built upon a few key concepts that ensure clarity, efficiency, and maintainability. Here's a brief overview:

Syntax and Structure of a Go Program:

Go programs are organized into packages. Every executable program starts with a main package containing a main() function. The language emphasizes a clean, minimal syntax that makes it straightforward to read and write code.

Variables, Constants, and Data Types:

Go is statically typed, meaning each variable's type is known at compile time. Variables can be declared using the var keyword or shorthand notation, while constants are defined with const. The language provides a range of basic data types including integers, floats, booleans, and strings, along with more complex types like arrays, slices, and maps.

Control Structures: If, For, Switch:

Control flow in Go is managed using familiar constructs. The if statement handles conditional logic, for serves as the sole looping construct (capable of handling what many languages do with while loops), and switch statements allow for clean multi-way branching without fall-through by default.

Functions and Packages:

Functions are first-class citizens in Go and are declared with the func keyword. They support multiple return values, which is particularly useful for error handling. Packages are used to organize code into reusable modules, with the standard library offering a rich collection of packages for various tasks.

Together, these basics form a robust framework that promotes writing clear, maintainable, and efficient code in Go.

2.1 Syntax and Structure of a Go Program

Go programs are organized around a simple yet powerful structure that emphasizes clarity and modularity. Here's an overview of the syntax and structure of a typical Go program:

1. Package Declaration

Every Go source file begins with a package declaration. This defines the package to which the file belongs. For executable programs, the package is usually named main:

```go
Copy code
package main
```

Packages allow you to organize and reuse code effectively across multiple files and projects.

2. Import Statements

After declaring the package, you specify the libraries your program depends on using import statements. Go's standard library is rich, and you can also import third-party packages:

```go
import (
    "fmt"   // Standard library package for formatted I/O
    "os"    // Standard library package for OS functions
)
```

The parentheses allow grouping multiple imports in a clean and organized manner.

3. The main Function

For an executable Go program, the entry point is the main function, defined within the main package. This function is automatically called when the program starts:

```go
func main() {
    fmt.Println("Hello, World!")
}
```

The main function serves as the starting point for program execution.

4. Function Declarations

Functions in Go are declared using the func keyword. Functions can accept parameters, return multiple values, and even be assigned to variables:

```go
Copy code
func add(a int, b int) int {
    return a + b
}
```

This concise syntax encourages writing clear and maintainable code.

5. Variable Declarations

Go supports both explicit and inferred variable declarations. Variables can be declared with the var keyword:

```go
Copy code
var count int = 10
```

Or using the shorthand syntax with :=, which infers the variable type:

```go
Copy code
name := "Go Developer"
```

Constants are declared similarly, using the const keyword:

```go
Copy code
const pi = 3.14159
```

6. Control Structures

Go offers a straightforward set of control structures:

Conditional Statements: if, else if, and else for decision-making.
Loops: The for loop is the sole looping construct, capable of handling simple loops, while loops, and range-based iterations:

```go
Copy code
for i := 0; i < 5; i++ {
    fmt.Println(i)
}
```

Switch Statements: Clean multi-branching without fall-through by default:

```go
Copy code
switch day := "Monday"; day {
case "Monday":
    fmt.Println("Start of the work week")
default:
    fmt.Println("Midweek or weekend")
}
```

7. Organizing Code into Files and Packages

In larger projects, code is split across multiple files and packages. Each file starts with a package declaration, and related functionalities are grouped together in packages. This modular design promotes code reuse and makes maintenance easier.

8. Comments

Go supports both single-line (//) and multi-line (/* ... */) comments. Well-documented code is a best practice, and Go even supports documentation generation using comments:

```go
Copy code
// add returns the sum of two integers.
func add(a int, b int) int {
    return a + b
}
```

Summary

The syntax and structure of a Go program are designed for simplicity and efficiency. Starting with a clear package declaration, followed by necessary imports, and culminating in a well-defined main function (for executables), Go encourages developers to write clean, modular, and maintainable code. Its concise function and variable declaration syntax, robust control structures, and emphasis on code organization make Go an excellent language for modern software development.

2.2 Variables, Constants, and Data Types

In Go, variables, constants, and data types form the backbone of how data is stored, manipulated, and enforced in your programs. Understanding these elements is crucial to writing clear, reliable, and efficient code.

Variables

Declaration and Initialization:

Variables in Go are explicitly declared with a type or implicitly declared with type inference. The primary keyword for variable declaration is var. For example:

```go
Copy code
var age int = 30
```

Go also supports shorthand notation using := when declaring and initializing a variable simultaneously:

```go
Copy code
name := "Alice"
```

This shorthand automatically infers the variable's type based on the assigned value.

Zero Values:

If a variable is declared without an explicit initial value, it automatically receives a zero value, which depends on the type. For instance:

Integers default to 0
Booleans default to false
Strings default to "" (an empty string)

Scope and Lifetime:

Variables declared inside functions are local to that function, while those declared outside are package-level variables accessible throughout the package. Understanding scope is key to managing the visibility and lifetime of data.

Constants

Definition and Usage:

Constants in Go are declared with the const keyword and, unlike variables, their values cannot be changed once set. This is useful for defining values that are meant to remain fixed throughout the program:

```go
Copy code
const pi = 3.14159
const greeting = "Hello, World!"
```

Constants can be character, string, boolean, or numeric values. They can also be used to create enumerated sets of related values.

Benefits of Constants:

Immutability: Once defined, their value remains constant, reducing the risk of accidental changes.

Self-Documentation: Constants can make your code more readable and maintainable by giving meaningful names to fixed values.

Data Types

Go is a statically typed language, which means that every variable has a specific data type known at compile time. The language supports several basic and composite data types:

Basic Types:

Integers: int, int8, int16, int32, int64, along with unsigned versions like uint, uint8, etc.
Floating-Point Numbers: float32 and float64
Boolean: bool
String: Represented by the string type, which is immutable.

Composite Types:

Arrays: Fixed-size collections of elements with the same type.
go
Copy code
```go
var numbers [5]int
```

Slices: Dynamic, flexible views into arrays. Slices are more commonly used than arrays in Go.
go
Copy code
```go
fruits := []string{"apple", "banana", "cherry"}
```

Maps: Key-value data structures for storing and retrieving data efficiently.

go
Copy code
```
capitals := map[string]string{"France": "Paris", "Japan": "Tokyo"}
```

Structs: Custom composite types that group together variables under a single name.

go
Copy code
```
type Person struct {
    Name string
    Age  int
}
person := Person{Name: "Bob", Age: 25}
```

Type Conversion:

Go requires explicit type conversion when assigning a value of one type to another. This helps prevent errors due to unintentional type mismatches:

```go
go
Copy code
var i int = 42
var f float64 = float64(i)
```

Type Inference and the Empty Interface:

While Go is statically typed, its ability to infer types using :=
simplifies coding without sacrificing type safety.
Additionally, the interface{} type can hold values of any
type, enabling polymorphic behavior:

```go
go
Copy code
var anyValue interface{} = "A string can be here"
```

Conclusion

In summary, Go's approach to variables, constants, and data
types is designed to enforce type safety and clarity while still
offering flexibility. Variables allow you to store mutable data,
constants provide reliable fixed values, and a robust set of
data types supports both simple and complex data
structures. This strong, statically typed foundation not only

helps catch errors at compile time but also leads to code that is easier to understand, maintain, and optimize.

2.3 Control Structures: If, For, Switch

Control structures in Go provide a straightforward and expressive way to control the flow of your program. The language supports three primary control structures for decision-making and looping: if, for, and switch. Each of these structures is designed with simplicity and clarity in mind.

1. The if Statement

Purpose:

The if statement allows your program to execute a block of code conditionally. It evaluates a boolean expression and runs the corresponding block if the condition is true.

Syntax and Features:

Basic Form:

go
Copy code

```
if condition {
    // code to execute when condition is true
}
```

With an else Block:

go
Copy code

```
if condition {
    // code for true condition
} else {
    // code for false condition
}
```

Multiple Conditions with else if:

go
Copy code

```
if condition1 {
    // code for condition1 being true
} else if condition2 {
```

```
    // code for condition2 being true
} else {
    // code if none of the above conditions are met
}
```

Optional Initialization Statement:

You can include an initialization statement before the condition, which is scoped to the if block:

go
Copy code
```go
if x := computeValue(); x > threshold {
    fmt.Println("x exceeds the threshold")
} else {
    fmt.Println("x is within the limit")
}
```

2. The for Loop

Purpose:
Go uses a single looping construct—the for loop—which can be used in various ways to iterate over data, repeat execution, or even mimic a traditional while loop.

Forms of the for Loop:

Traditional For Loop: This form is similar to loops found in languages like C or Java:

go
Copy code

```
for i := 0; i < 10; i++ {
    fmt.Println(i)
}
```

While-like Loop: Omit the initialization and post statements to create a loop that continues while a condition is true:

go
Copy code

```
i := 0
for i < 10 {
    fmt.Println(i)
    i++
}
```

Infinite Loop: When no condition is specified, the loop runs indefinitely until interrupted by a break or another control mechanism:

go
Copy code

```go
for {
    // repeated execution until an explicit break is
    encountered
    if someCondition() {
        break
    }
}
```

Range-Based Loop: The range keyword allows you to iterate over arrays, slices, maps, or strings conveniently:

go
Copy code

```go
numbers := []int{10, 20, 30}
for index, value := range numbers {
    fmt.Printf("Index: %d, Value: %d\n", index, value)
}
```

3. The switch Statement

Purpose:

The switch statement in Go is used for multi-way branch selection, offering a more readable and maintainable alternative to a series of if-else statements.

Syntax and Features:

Basic Structure:
```go
Copy code
switch variable {
case value1:
    // code for value1
case value2:
    // code for value2
default:
    // code if no cases match
}
```

No Implicit Fallthrough:

Unlike some languages, Go's switch statement does not automatically fall through from one case to the next. If you want to continue to the next case, you must explicitly use the fallthrough keyword.

Expressionless Switch:

You can omit the switch expression and use it as a cleaner way to handle complex conditionals:

```go
go
Copy code
switch {
case condition1:
    fmt.Println("Condition1 is true")
case condition2:
    fmt.Println("Condition2 is true")
default:
    fmt.Println("No conditions met")
}
```

Initialization in Switch:

Similar to the if statement, you can include an initialization statement:

```go
go
Copy code
switch x := computeValue(); {
case x < 0:
    fmt.Println("Negative value")
case x == 0:
    fmt.Println("Zero value")
default:
    fmt.Println("Positive value")
}
```

Summary

if Statements:

Allow you to execute code blocks based on conditions, with support for initialization and multiple branching via else if and else.

for Loops:

The single loop construct in Go is highly versatile, supporting traditional for loops, while-like loops, infinite loops, and range-based iterations.

switch Statements:

Provide a clean, efficient way to handle multi-way branch selection without the pitfalls of fall-through, unless explicitly desired.

These control structures in Go are designed to be simple and expressive, enabling you to write clear, concise, and efficient code that handles complex logical flows with ease.

2.4 Functions and Packages

In Go, functions and packages are two fundamental building blocks that help you write modular, reusable, and maintainable code. Below is an overview of both concepts.

Functions

Functions in Go are declared using the func keyword and provide a way to encapsulate code into reusable units. They play a central role in structuring your code and are used for everything from simple tasks to complex logic.

Key Aspects of Functions

Declaration and Syntax:

A basic function declaration includes the function name, a list of parameters (each with a type), and the return type(s). For example:

```go
Copy code
func add(a int, b int) int {
    return a + b
}
```

Multiple Return Values:

One of Go's distinctive features is its support for functions returning multiple values. This is especially useful for returning a result along with an error.

```go
Copy code
func divide(dividend, divisor float64) (float64, error) {
    if divisor == 0 {
        return 0, fmt.Errorf("cannot divide by zero")
    }
    return dividend / divisor, nil
}
```

Variadic Functions:

Functions can accept a variable number of arguments using the ellipsis (...) notation.

```go
Copy code
func sum(numbers ...int) int {
    total := 0
    for _, number := range numbers {
        total += number
    }
    return total
}
```

Anonymous Functions and Closures:

Go supports anonymous functions, which can be defined inline and even assigned to variables. These functions can capture variables from the surrounding context.

```go
Copy code
func main() {
    greet := func(name string) string {
        return "Hello, " + name
    }
    fmt.Println(greet("Go Developer"))
}
```

Method Receivers:

In Go, you can define methods on types, enabling object-like behavior. Methods are functions with a receiver argument.

```go
Copy code
type Rectangle struct {
    Width, Height float64
}

func (r Rectangle) Area() float64 {
    return r.Width * r.Height
}
```

Packages

Packages are the way Go organizes code into reusable modules. They help separate functionality into logical units and provide encapsulation.

Key Aspects of Packages

Package Declaration:

Every Go source file starts with a package declaration. For executable programs, the package name is main, and for libraries or reusable code, you choose a descriptive package name.

go
Copy code
```go
// File: mathutils.go
package mathutils

func Multiply(a, b int) int {
    return a * b
}
```

Exported vs. Unexported Identifiers:

In Go, an identifier (such as a function or variable) is exported from a package if its name starts with an uppercase letter. Unexported identifiers (starting with a lowercase letter) remain private to the package.

go
Copy code

```go
// Exported function
func PublicFunction() {
    // accessible from other packages
}

// Unexported function
func privateFunction() {
    // accessible only within the package
}
```

Importing Packages:

To use functions, types, or variables from another package, you import it using the import statement.

```go
go
Copy code
package main

import (
    "fmt"
    "your_module/mathutils" // replace with the correct module path
)
```

```go
func main() {
    result := mathutils.Multiply(3, 4)
    fmt.Println("3 multiplied by 4 is:", result)
}
```

Package Initialization:

Go packages can include an init() function that executes before the main function or before the package is used. This is useful for setting up initial state.

```go
go
Copy code
package config

var AppName string

func init() {
    AppName = "MyGoApp"
}
```

Modular Code Organization:

With Go modules (introduced in Go 1.11 and enabled by default in later versions), managing dependencies and versioning becomes simpler. You can initialize a new module with:

```bash
Copy code
go mod init your_module_name
```

Summary

Functions in Go are defined using the func keyword and can accept parameters, return multiple values, and even be used as anonymous functions. They allow you to encapsulate logic and promote code reuse.

Packages help you organize code into logical units. They facilitate code reuse and maintainability by enabling you to separate functionalities, control visibility through exported and unexported identifiers, and manage dependencies via Go modules.

Together, functions and packages provide a robust framework for building scalable and maintainable Go applications, fostering a clean separation of concerns and efficient code organization.

Chapter 3
Working with Data

Working with data in Go involves a variety of built-in types and constructs that allow you to represent, manipulate, and exchange information efficiently. Here's a brief overview:

Arrays, Slices, and Maps:

Arrays provide fixed-size collections of elements of the same type, while slices offer a dynamic, flexible view into arrays, making them the preferred choice for most tasks. Maps, on the other hand, store key-value pairs, enabling fast lookups and efficient data organization.

Structs and Custom Types:

Structs allow you to define complex, composite data types by grouping related fields together. They are essential for modeling real-world entities and creating custom types that reflect the structure of your data.

Pointers and Memory Management:

Pointers in Go hold the memory addresses of variables, providing a means to reference and modify data efficiently. While Go handles memory management through garbage collection, understanding pointers is key to optimizing performance and managing data structures.

JSON Encoding and Decoding:

Go's standard library includes the encoding/json package, which makes it straightforward to convert data structures to and from JSON format. This feature is particularly useful for web development and API interactions, where JSON is a common data interchange format.

Together, these features enable you to work with data in a clear, efficient, and type-safe manner, laying a solid foundation for building robust applications.

3.1 Arrays, Slices, and Maps

Arrays, slices, and maps are fundamental data structures in Go that help you store and manage collections of data. Each offers its own characteristics and use cases, making them valuable tools in a Go programmer's toolkit.

Arrays

Definition and Characteristics:

Fixed Size: An array in Go has a fixed length defined at compile time. This means once an array is declared, its size cannot change.
Homogeneous Elements: All elements in an array must be of the same type.

Declaration and Initialization:

Arrays are declared by specifying the size and type. For example:

```go
Copy code
var numbers [5]int
```

You can also initialize an array with values:

```go
```

Copy code

```
primes := [5]int{2, 3, 5, 7, 11}
```

Alternatively, you can let Go determine the size based on the number of initializer elements:

go
Copy code

```
colors := [...]string{"red", "green", "blue"}
```

Usage Considerations:

Arrays are useful when the number of elements is known and fixed.
Because they are value types, assigning an array to another variable creates a copy of all its elements.
Slices

Definition and Characteristics:

Dynamic and Flexible: Slices are built on top of arrays but provide a more flexible, dynamic interface. Their length can grow or shrink as needed.
Underlying Array: A slice is a reference to a segment of an underlying array. Modifications to the slice may affect the underlying array.

Declaration and Initialization:

You can create a slice by slicing an array or by using a literal:

go
Copy code
```
numbers := []int{1, 2, 3, 4, 5}
```

Slices can also be created from an existing array:

go
Copy code
```
arr := [5]int{10, 20, 30, 40, 50}
slice := arr[1:4] // Contains elements 20, 30, 40
```
Key Properties:

Length and Capacity:

The length of a slice is the number of elements it contains. The capacity is the size of the underlying array starting from the slice's first element. You can obtain these using:

go
Copy code
```
fmt.Println(len(slice)) // Length of the slice
fmt.Println(cap(slice)) // Capacity of the slice
```

Appending Elements:

The append function is used to add elements to a slice:
go
Copy code
slice = append(slice, 60, 70)

If the underlying array is not large enough to accommodate new elements, Go automatically allocates a larger array and copies the elements over.

Iteration:

You can iterate over slices using the range keyword:
go
Copy code
```
for index, value := range numbers {
    fmt.Printf("Index: %d, Value: %d\n", index, value)
}
```

Maps

Definition and Characteristics:

Key-Value Store: Maps in Go are unordered collections that associate keys with values. They provide efficient lookup, insertion, and deletion of elements.

Dynamic Size: Unlike arrays, maps can grow and shrink dynamically as you add or remove key-value pairs.

Declaration and Initialization:

You declare a map by specifying the key and value types:
go
Copy code
```go
var capitals map[string]string
```

However, before you use a map, you need to initialize it using the make function:
go
Copy code
```go
capitals = make(map[string]string)
capitals["France"] = "Paris"
capitals["Japan"] = "Tokyo"
```

Alternatively, you can initialize a map with values using a

map literal:

go
Copy code

```go
colors := map[string]string{
    "red":   "#FF0000",
    "green": "#00FF00",
    "blue":  "#0000FF",
}
```

Common Operations:

Insertion/Update:
go
Copy code

```go
capitals["Germany"] = "Berlin"
```

Lookup and Existence Check:

When retrieving a value, you can check if the key exists:
go
Copy code

```go
if capital, ok := capitals["France"]; ok {
    fmt.Println("The capital of France is", capital)
} else {
    fmt.Println("Capital not found")
}
```

Deletion:

Remove a key-value pair using the delete function:
go
Copy code
delete(capitals, "Japan")

Iteration:

.Iterate over all key-value pairs using range:
go
Copy code
```
for country, city := range capitals {
    fmt.Printf("%s: %s\n", country, city)
}
```

Summary

Arrays are fixed in size and store elements of a single type. They are useful when the collection size is known in advance.

Slices offer a dynamic and flexible interface over arrays, providing powerful capabilities such as automatic resizing and easy slicing of data.

Maps provide an efficient key-value storage mechanism for data, with dynamic size and built-in support for fast lookups, insertion, and deletion.

Understanding when and how to use these data structures is essential for writing efficient and maintainable Go code. They form the basis for more complex data manipulations and are key to building robust applications.

3.2 Structs and Custom Types

In Go, structs and custom types are essential constructs that enable you to model real-world data and add semantic meaning to your code. They are central to organizing data in a clean, modular fashion and allow you to encapsulate both state and behavior.

Structs

Definition and Purpose:

A struct in Go is a composite data type that groups together variables (called fields) under a single name. Each field in a struct can have its own type, and together they form a blueprint for modeling more complex entities.

Syntax:

Defining a struct involves using the type keyword followed by the struct name and its fields:

```go
Copy code
type Person struct {
    Name string
    Age  int
}
```

In this example, the Person struct represents an individual with a Name and an Age.

Usage:

Once defined, you can create instances of the struct and access or modify its fields:

```go
Copy code
func main() {
    // Creating an instance of Person
    p := Person{Name: "Alice", Age: 30}

    // Accessing fields
    fmt.Println("Name:", p.Name)
    fmt.Println("Age:", p.Age)

    // Modifying fields
    p.Age = 31
}
```

Methods on Structs:

You can define methods with a receiver of a struct type to encapsulate behavior along with the data. This is similar to how methods work in object-oriented programming:

```go
Copy code
```

```go
func (p Person) Greet() {
    fmt.Printf("Hello, my name is %s and I am %d years old.\n", p.Name, p.Age)
}
```

Here, Greet is a method on the Person struct that prints a greeting message.

Custom Types

Creating Custom Types:

Beyond structs, Go allows you to define custom types using the type keyword. This enables you to create new types that are based on existing ones, adding clarity and intent to your code. For example, you might define a custom type for representing an age:

go
Copy code
```go
type Age int
```

This creates a new type Age that is distinct from the built-in int, even though its underlying representation is the same.

Type Aliases vs. New Types:

New Types:

When you define a new type (as shown above), it is considered a distinct type, and you must use explicit conversion when necessary.

Type Aliases:

Go also supports type aliases using the = syntax:
go
Copy code
type MyInt = int

This does not create a new type but merely provides another name for the existing type int.

Benefits of Custom Types:

Improved Readability: Custom types can give more context to your variables. For instance, distinguishing between a user ID and a product ID even if both are represented by integers.

Encapsulation of Behavior: By defining methods on a custom type, you can encapsulate behavior that is specific to that type. This enhances code organization and reuse.

Type Safety: Custom types help prevent accidental misuse of data by enforcing type checks at compile time.

Example – Using a Custom Type in a Struct:

```go
Copy code
type Age int

type Person struct {
    Name string
    Age  Age
}

func (p Person) IsAdult() bool {
    return p.Age >= 18
}

func main() {
    p := Person{Name: "Bob", Age: 20}
    if p.IsAdult() {
        fmt.Println(p.Name, "is an adult.")
```

```
    }
}
```

In this example, Age is a custom type, and a method IsAdult
is defined on Person to encapsulate logic related to age.

Summary

Structs provide a way to create composite types that group
related fields together, making it easier to model complex
data entities.
Custom Types allow you to define new types based on
existing ones, improving code clarity, type safety, and
enabling you to attach methods that encapsulate behavior.
Together, structs and custom types form a powerful
foundation in Go for writing organized, maintainable, and
expressive code.

3.3 Pointers and Memory Management

Pointers and memory management are crucial concepts in Go, enabling you to efficiently manage data and optimize application performance while maintaining safety. Go strikes a balance between low-level memory control and high-level simplicity, making it accessible for both beginners and experienced developers.

Pointers in Go

What Are Pointers?

Pointers are variables that store the memory address of another variable. Instead of holding data directly, a pointer refers to the location in memory where the actual data resides. This mechanism allows for more efficient data manipulation, particularly when dealing with large structures or when you need to modify a variable within a function.

Declaring and Initializing Pointers:

Declaration:

Use the asterisk (*) to declare a pointer variable that will hold the address of a specific type:

go
Copy code
var ptr *int

Initialization:

To assign a pointer the address of a variable, use the address-of operator (&):
go
Copy code
var number int = 42
ptr = &number

Dereferencing:

The dereference operator (*) is used to access or modify the value at the pointer's address:
go
Copy code
fmt.Println(*ptr) // Outputs: 42
*ptr = 100   // Changes the value of number to 100

Safety Considerations:

No Pointer Arithmetic:

Go deliberately avoids pointer arithmetic, a common source of bugs and security vulnerabilities in other languages like C or C++. This design choice promotes memory safety by preventing accidental pointer miscalculations.

Explicit Use:

While pointers allow direct memory access, they should be used judiciously. For many cases, passing values by copy is sufficient and simpler, especially for small data types.

Memory Management in Go

Garbage Collection:

One of Go's standout features is its built-in garbage collector. This system automatically tracks and reclaims memory that is no longer in use, reducing the likelihood of memory leaks and simplifying development. With garbage collection, developers do not have to manually free memory, which minimizes errors like dangling pointers and use-after-free issues.

Key Points About Go's Memory Management:

Automatic Memory Reclamation:

The garbage collector continuously monitors memory usage and recycles memory that becomes unreachable, allowing you to focus on application logic rather than manual memory deallocation.

Efficient Performance:

Go's garbage collector is designed to minimize pauses and impact on application performance, making it well-suited for both small programs and large, high-throughput applications.

Best Practices:

Use Pointers When Necessary:

Pointers can enhance performance by avoiding costly copies of large data structures. However, they should be used only when necessary.

Manage Concurrency Carefully:

When pointers are used in concurrent applications, proper synchronization mechanisms—such as mutexes or channels—must be implemented to prevent race conditions.

Profiling Tools:

Go provides profiling tools (e.g., pprof) that can help you analyze memory usage and optimize performance.

Summary

Pointers allow you to work directly with memory addresses, facilitating efficient data manipulation and function parameter passing without copying large structures. Their usage is safe in Go due to the language's deliberate avoidance of pointer arithmetic and clear syntax.

Memory Management is largely handled by Go's garbage collector, which automates the process of memory reclamation. This automatic memory management reduces common errors associated with manual memory handling and allows developers to concentrate on writing clean, efficient code.

Together, pointers and Go's memory management features provide the control needed for performance-critical applications while maintaining a high level of safety and simplicity in your code.

3.4 JSON Encoding and Decoding

Go provides built-in support for working with JSON—a widely used data interchange format—through its encoding/json package. This package makes it easy to convert Go data structures to JSON (encoding) and JSON data back into Go data structures (decoding). Here's an overview of how JSON encoding and decoding work in Go:

1. JSON Encoding

Purpose:

Encoding is the process of converting Go values into JSON format. This is particularly useful when you need to send data over HTTP, store configuration files, or interact with APIs that use JSON.

Using json.Marshal:

Basic Usage:

The json.Marshal function converts a Go value into a JSON-formatted byte slice. For example, given a struct:

```go
Copy code
type Person struct {
    Name string `json:"name"`
    Age  int    `json:"age"`
}

func main() {
    p := Person{Name: "Alice", Age: 30}
    jsonData, err := json.Marshal(p)
    if err != nil {
        log.Fatalf("Error encoding JSON: %v", err)
    }
    fmt.Println(string(jsonData))
}
```

In this example, the struct is annotated with JSON field tags to control the key names in the resulting JSON. The output might look like:

json
Copy code
{"name":"Alice","age":30}

Pretty Printing:

If you prefer human-readable output, you can use json.MarshalIndent:

go
Copy code
```go
jsonData, err := json.MarshalIndent(p, "", "  ")
if err != nil {
    log.Fatalf("Error encoding JSON: %v", err)
}
fmt.Println(string(jsonData))
```

2. JSON Decoding

Purpose:

Decoding is the process of converting JSON data into Go values. This is essential when reading data from an API response, file, or any external source in JSON format.

Using json.Unmarshal:

Basic Usage:

The json.Unmarshal function converts JSON data (a byte slice) into a Go value. Consider the following example:

```go
Copy code
func main() {
    jsonData := []byte(`{"name":"Alice","age":30}`)
    var p Person
    err := json.Unmarshal(jsonData, &p)
    if err != nil {
        log.Fatalf("Error decoding JSON: %v", err)
    }
    fmt.Printf("Decoded Person: %+v\n", p)
}
```

Here, the JSON data is parsed into a Person struct. Notice that the address of p is passed so that json.Unmarshal can modify it with the decoded data.

Decoding into Maps or Interface Types:

Sometimes, you might not have a predefined struct. In such cases, you can decode JSON into a map[string]interface{} or an empty interface (interface{}), which provides flexibility at the cost of type safety:

```go
Copy code
var result map[string]interface{}
err := json.Unmarshal(jsonData, &result)
if err != nil {
    log.Fatalf("Error decoding JSON: %v", err)
}
fmt.Println(result)
```

3. Customizing JSON Behavior

Field Tags:

You can control JSON encoding/decoding behavior using struct field tags. For example, to omit fields or change key names:

go
Copy code

```go
type Person struct {
    Name string `json:"full_name"`
    Age  int    `json:"age,omitempty"` // 'omitempty' omits the field if it's the zero value
}
```

Custom Marshal/Unmarshal Methods:

If you need more control, you can define custom methods by implementing the json.Marshaler and json.Unmarshaler interfaces. This is useful for types that require special formatting or handling during the encoding or decoding process.

Summary

Encoding:

Use json.Marshal (or json.MarshalIndent for formatted output) to convert Go values to JSON. Annotate struct fields with JSON tags to control key names and behavior.

Decoding:

Use json.Unmarshal to convert JSON data into Go values. Decode into structs for type safety or into maps/interfaces for flexibility.

The encoding/json package in Go streamlines the process of working with JSON data, making it straightforward to integrate with web services, APIs, and other systems that rely on JSON for data exchange.

Part II: Writing Clean and Efficient Code

Chapter 4
Writing Idiomatic Go

Writing idiomatic Go means writing code that not only works but also aligns with the language's philosophy and community standards. Here are some key aspects:

Clarity and Simplicity:

Go emphasizes straightforward, easy-to-read code. Avoid unnecessary complexity or clever hacks; instead, prefer clear, explicit constructs. This often means writing code that may be a few lines longer but is far easier to understand and maintain.

Effective Naming Conventions:

Use descriptive names for functions, variables, and types. Follow Go's convention where exported names start with an uppercase letter (making them public) while unexported ones remain lowercase. Consistent naming helps signal the intended use and scope of identifiers.

Error Handling:

Go opts for explicit error handling over exceptions. Check errors immediately after function calls and handle them appropriately. This pattern—returning error values as the last return parameter—is a cornerstone of idiomatic Go and improves code robustness.

Standard Library and Built-in Tools:

Leverage Go's rich standard library and built-in tools such as go fmt for formatting, go vet for static analysis, and go test for testing. Using these tools helps maintain consistency across codebases and catches common pitfalls early.

Minimalism in Design:

Avoid over-engineering. Idiomatic Go code favors simple, pragmatic solutions. Instead of complex inheritance or overuse of design patterns, use interfaces and composition to achieve flexibility without sacrificing clarity.

By following these practices, you ensure that your Go code is not only functional but also clean, maintainable, and easily understood by other developers in the community.

4.1 Effective Go: Best Practices

Effective Go" is both a philosophy and a set of guidelines that help developers write clear, maintainable, and efficient Go code. Following these best practices not only leads to robust software but also ensures that your code remains accessible to other developers in the community. Here are some key principles:

1. Clarity and Simplicity

Keep It Simple:

Favor straightforward, easy-to-read code over clever or overly abstract solutions. Simple code is more maintainable and less prone to errors.

Small, Focused Functions:
Write functions that do one thing well. Small functions are easier to test, debug, and reuse.

2. Naming Conventions

Descriptive Names:

Choose clear and descriptive names for variables, functions, and types. Names should convey intent, making the code self-documenting.

Exported vs. Unexported:

Follow Go's convention where identifiers that start with an uppercase letter are exported (public) and those starting with a lowercase letter are unexported (private). This practice helps define clear package interfaces.

3. Explicit Error Handling

Check Errors Immediately:

Go uses explicit error returns instead of exceptions. Always check errors immediately after a function call and handle them appropriately.

Propagate Meaningful Errors:

When returning errors, provide context to make debugging easier. Consider using custom error types or wrapping errors to add additional information.

4. Leverage the Standard Library and Tools

Use gofmt and go vet:

Format your code with gofmt to maintain consistency and readability. Use go vet to catch common mistakes before they become bugs.

Standard Library First:

Before turning to third-party packages, explore Go's rich standard library. It often provides reliable and efficient implementations for common tasks.

5. Idiomatic Use of Language Features

Slices Over Arrays:
Prefer slices for collections since they offer flexibility with dynamic sizing.

Defer for Cleanup:
Use the defer statement to ensure resources are properly released (e.g., closing files or unlocking mutexes) even when errors occur.

Effective Use of Concurrency:

Leverage goroutines and channels to simplify concurrent programming. When sharing data, use synchronization primitives like mutexes and always be mindful of potential race conditions—tools like the race detector can help identify issues.

6. Package Organization and API Design

Modular Code:

Organize your code into packages that encapsulate related functionality. A well-structured package makes it easier to reuse code and maintain a clear separation of concerns.

Minimal and Clear APIs:

Expose only what is necessary. Keep package APIs simple and focused, hiding implementation details to reduce coupling and improve maintainability.

7. Testing and Documentation

Write Tests:

Incorporate unit tests and integration tests to ensure your code behaves as expected. Go's testing framework makes it easy to write and run tests.

Document Your Code:

Use comments and Go's documentation conventions to explain the "why" behind your code. Good documentation helps others (and your future self) understand your design decisions.

8. Performance Awareness

Profile When Necessary:

Use profiling tools like pprof to identify bottlenecks. Focus on optimizing parts of the code that truly affect performance.

Avoid Premature Optimization:

Write clean and correct code first. Optimize only when measurements indicate a need, ensuring that performance improvements do not come at the cost of readability.

Conclusion

Effective Go is about writing code that is not only functional but also elegant and idiomatic. By emphasizing clarity, explicit error handling, modular design, and leveraging Go's robust standard library and tools, you create software that is easier to maintain, extend, and collaborate on. These best practices form the backbone of a Go codebase that stands the test of time and scales gracefully with your project's needs.

4.2 Error Handling in Go

Error handling in Go is designed to be explicit, straightforward, and an integral part of program logic rather than an afterthought. Unlike languages that rely on exceptions, Go functions that might encounter errors return an additional value—typically of type error—which callers are expected to check and handle immediately.

Key Aspects of Error Handling in Go

Explicit Error Returns:

Functions that can fail usually return an error as their last return value. For example:

```go
Copy code
func readFile(filename string) ([]byte, error) {
    data, err := os.ReadFile(filename)
```

```go
    if err != nil {
        return nil, err
    }
    return data, nil
}
```

This explicit design forces the caller to consider the possibility of failure, leading to more robust error handling.

Immediate Error Checking:

It is idiomatic in Go to check errors right after they are returned:

```go
go
Copy code
data, err := readFile("example.txt")
if err != nil {
    log.Fatalf("Failed to read file: %v", err)
}
// Proceed with using data...
```

This pattern helps prevent errors from being inadvertently ignored.

The error Interface:

In Go, the error type is a built-in interface:

```go
Copy code
type error interface {
    Error() string
}
```

Any type that implements the Error() method satisfies the error interface, allowing developers to create custom error types that can carry additional context or behavior.

Error Wrapping and Unwrapping:

Since Go 1.13, the standard library includes functionality for wrapping errors with additional context using fmt.Errorf and the %w verb:

```go
Copy code
if err := someFunc(); err != nil {
    return fmt.Errorf("someFunc failed: %w", err)
}
```

This wrapped error can later be unwrapped or inspected using functions from the errors package (e.g., errors.Is or errors.As), enabling more sophisticated error handling strategies.

Custom Error Types:

Creating custom error types allows you to attach additional data to errors and differentiate between error kinds:

```go
Copy code
type NotFoundError struct {
    Resource string
}

func (e *NotFoundError) Error() string {
    return fmt.Sprintf("%s not found", e.Resource)
}
```

Callers can then use type assertions to handle specific error types differently.

Avoiding Panics for Regular Error Handling:

Go encourages developers to handle errors gracefully instead of using panics for expected error conditions. Panics are reserved for unrecoverable situations where the program cannot continue safely.

Error Propagation:

When a function encounters an error, it often propagates that error up the call stack rather than handling it immediately. This propagation allows higher-level functions, which have more context about the overall operation, to decide how best to react.

Best Practices

Always Check Errors:

Never ignore returned errors. Even if you're confident an error won't occur, it's better to be safe and check explicitly.

Provide Context:

When returning an error, add context to make debugging easier. Wrapped errors provide a trace of what went wrong at each level of the call stack.

Keep Error Messages Clear:

Write error messages that are concise yet informative. Avoid overly generic messages; instead, indicate what operation failed and why.

Use the errors Package:

Utilize errors.Is and errors.As for comparing and extracting information from errors. This makes your error handling more robust and future-proof.

Summary

Error handling in Go emphasizes clarity and explicitness. By requiring functions to return errors and by promoting immediate error checking, Go helps developers write programs that are resilient and easier to debug. With tools for error wrapping and custom error types, Go's approach allows for detailed and context-rich error reporting while maintaining a simple and understandable error-handling paradigm.

4.3 Writing Clean and Readable Code

Writing clean and readable code is a cornerstone of effective software development, and Go's design philosophy actively supports this goal. Clean code is not only easier to understand and maintain but also reduces the likelihood of bugs. Below are some key principles and best practices for writing clean and readable Go code:

1. Follow a Consistent Style

Use gofmt:

Go provides the gofmt tool to automatically format your code. Running gofmt ensures that your code adheres to a standard style, making it easier for others (and your future self) to read and understand.

Consistent Naming Conventions:

Use descriptive names for variables, functions, and types. Follow Go's convention where exported names begin with an uppercase letter and unexported names with a lowercase letter. This clarity helps others quickly grasp the purpose of your code.

2. Write Small, Focused Functions
Single Responsibility:

Each function should perform one clear task. Small, focused functions are easier to test, debug, and reuse.

Clear Interfaces:

Design functions with explicit inputs and outputs. Avoid hidden side effects by passing all necessary data through parameters and returning results directly.

3. Organize Your Code Well

Use Packages Wisely:

Group related functionality into packages. A well-organized package structure not only promotes reusability but also clarifies the boundaries between different parts of your application.

Modular Design:

Break your application into logical modules. This modularity makes the codebase easier to navigate and maintain.

4. Document Your Code
Comment with Purpose:

Use comments to explain why something is done rather than what is done, especially when the code's purpose isn't immediately obvious.

Leverage Go's Documentation Tools:

Use Go's built-in documentation format by writing comments above package declarations, functions, and types. This practice not only aids human readers but also integrates with Go's documentation generation tools.

5. Embrace Idiomatic Constructs

Error Handling:

Write explicit error-handling code. By checking and propagating errors immediately, you prevent hidden bugs and make the control flow clear.

Effective Use of Language Features:

Utilize Go's slices, maps, and interfaces appropriately. Avoid over-complicating code with unnecessary abstractions; instead, rely on the language's simplicity and clarity.

Defer for Cleanup:

Use the defer statement to handle cleanup operations, such as closing files or unlocking mutexes. This ensures that resources are properly released, even when errors occur.

6. Keep It Simple

Avoid Overengineering:

Simple, straightforward solutions are often more robust than complex ones. When faced with a problem, start with the simplest solution that could possibly work.

Readable Logic Flow:

Structure your code so that its flow is easy to follow. Clear conditional logic and proper error handling contribute to a readable codebase.

Conclusion

Writing clean and readable code in Go is a blend of using the language's robust features, adhering to its conventions, and following sound software design principles. By using tools like gofmt, writing small and focused functions, organizing your code into logical packages, documenting effectively, and embracing idiomatic practices, you can create code that is not only efficient but also a pleasure to read and maintain. This focus on clarity and simplicity not only benefits individual developers but also enhances team collaboration and long-term project success.

4.4 Code Organization and Project Structure

Effective code organization and a well-thought-out project structure are essential for developing maintainable, scalable, and collaborative Go applications. By structuring your code logically and modularly, you make it easier for yourself and others to navigate, understand, and extend your project over time. Here are some key aspects to consider:

1. Use of Packages

Modularity and Reusability:

In Go, packages are the primary means of organizing code. Each package encapsulates a related set of functionalities, helping you enforce separation of concerns. A well-defined package has a clear public API and hides its internal implementation details.

Naming Conventions:

Package names should be short, descriptive, and written in lowercase without underscores or mixed caps. Consistent naming makes it easier to import and use packages across your project.

Exported vs. Unexported:

Only identifiers (functions, types, variables, etc.) that start with an uppercase letter are accessible outside the package. This allows you to expose only what's necessary and maintain control over your package's internal workings.

2. Project Structure with Go Modules

Module Initialization:

With the introduction of Go modules, you can initialize your project with a go.mod file using go mod init <module-name>. This file manages your dependencies and defines your module's path.

Directory Layout:

Although Go does not enforce a specific directory structure, many projects follow common conventions:

cmd/ Directory:

Contains the entry points for your application. Each subdirectory in cmd/ typically corresponds to a different executable. For example, cmd/server might contain the main package for your server application.

pkg/ Directory:

Houses libraries and packages that are meant to be consumed by other applications. This directory is used for code that you intend to be imported by external projects.

internal/ Directory:

Contains packages that are private to your project. Code in the internal/ directory cannot be imported by external modules, which reinforces encapsulation and reduces the risk of unintended dependencies.

Other Common Directories:

api/: Definitions for API interfaces, handlers, or client implementations.
configs/: Configuration files and templates.
scripts/: Build, deployment, or automation scripts.
test/: Additional external test data or integration tests.

Vendor Directory (Optional):

While Go modules handle dependency management automatically, some projects choose to use a vendor/ directory to store copies of external dependencies. This can help ensure reproducible builds, although it is optional in modern Go development.

3. Guidelines for Code Organization

Single Responsibility Principle:
Each package and function should have a clear, focused purpose. This not only improves code readability but also makes testing and maintenance easier.

Avoid Cyclic Dependencies:

Organize packages such that they remain independent of one another. Cyclic dependencies can lead to complications in code reuse and testing.

Documentation and Comments:

Document packages, public functions, and types using Go's documentation conventions. Clear documentation helps onboard new contributors and clarifies the intent behind code organization.

Testing Strategy:

Place test files in the same package as the code they test (e.g., foo_test.go). This keeps tests close to the source code and simplifies dependency management.

4. Benefits of a Well-Organized Codebase

Improved Maintainability:

A clear structure makes it easier to locate files, understand dependencies, and modify or extend functionality.

Enhanced Collaboration:

Consistent code organization promotes a common understanding among team members, reducing onboarding time and minimizing miscommunication.

Scalability:

A modular project structure supports growth. As your project expands, having well-separated packages and directories helps in managing complexity and allows for easier refactoring.

Conclusion

Investing time in planning your project's structure and adhering to best practices for code organization can pay significant dividends as your codebase grows. By leveraging Go's package system, adopting a clear directory layout (with directories like cmd, pkg, and internal), and following principles such as the single responsibility principle and avoiding cyclic dependencies, you create a robust, scalable foundation for your Go applications. This approach not only improves maintainability but also facilitates collaboration and long-term success in your development projects.

Chapter 5
Testing and Debugging

Testing and debugging are integral parts of developing robust Go applications. Go offers a built-in testing framework and a variety of tools that simplify both unit testing and the debugging process.

Testing in Go

The testing Package:

Go's standard library includes the testing package, which enables you to write unit tests as functions that begin with Test (e.g., TestFunctionName). Running go test in your project directory automatically finds and executes these test functions.

Table-Driven Tests:

A common pattern in Go is table-driven testing. This approach involves defining a slice of test cases—each with its own input and expected output—and then iterating over the slice to validate your code. This pattern makes it easy to add new test cases and improves test clarity.

Benchmarking:

For performance evaluation, you can write benchmarks using functions that begin with Benchmark and utilize the testing.B type. Running go test -bench=. executes these benchmarks, helping you identify performance bottlenecks.

Debugging in Go
Print Debugging and Logging:

A straightforward approach to debugging in Go is to insert print statements or use logging (with packages like log or third-party libraries) to trace code execution and inspect variable values.

Delve Debugger:

For more sophisticated debugging, the Delve debugger is a popular choice. It provides features like breakpoints, step execution, and variable inspection, making it easier to diagnose issues in real time.

Profiling Tools:

Go also includes powerful profiling tools such as pprof for CPU and memory profiling. These tools help identify performance issues and memory leaks by generating detailed profiles that you can analyze using visualization tools.

Best Practices

Write Comprehensive Tests:

Aim to cover critical paths in your code with tests, including edge cases and error conditions. Well-written tests not only verify functionality but also serve as documentation for expected behavior.

Automate Testing:

Integrate tests into your continuous integration pipeline to ensure that new changes do not break existing functionality.

Iterative Debugging:

When debugging, isolate problematic sections of code by testing components individually. Use logging judiciously to minimize noise and focus on the issue at hand.

By leveraging Go's testing framework and debugging tools, you can build and maintain high-quality, performant applications while reducing the time spent on troubleshooting issues.

5.1 Writing Unit Tests with testing Package

Go's built-in testing package provides a simple yet powerful framework for writing unit tests. Unit tests help verify that individual pieces of your code work as expected, catching bugs early and ensuring that future changes don't break functionality. Here's an overview of writing unit tests using the testing package in Go:

1. Creating a Test File

Naming Convention:

Test files must be named with the _test.go suffix (e.g., math_test.go). This convention ensures that the Go toolchain recognizes and runs the file during testing.

Test Functions:

Each test function should start with the prefix Test followed by a descriptive name. They must accept a single parameter of type *testing.T:

```go
Copy code
func TestAdd(t *testing.T) {
    // test code goes here
```

```go
}
```

2. Writing a Simple Unit Test

Suppose you have a simple function to add two integers:

```go
Copy code
// File: math.go
package math

func Add(a, b int) int {
    return a + b
}
```

You can write a corresponding unit test as follows:

```go
Copy code
// File: math_test.go
package math

import "testing"

func TestAdd(t *testing.T) {
```

```go
    result := Add(2, 3)
    expected := 5
    if result != expected {
        t.Errorf("Add(2, 3) = %d; want %d", result, expected)
    }
}
```

In this example, if the actual result does not match the expected value, the test fails and reports an error using t.Errorf.

3. Table-Driven Tests

A common pattern in Go is the table-driven test, where you define a list of test cases and iterate over them. This makes it easy to add new test scenarios and keeps your tests organized:

go
Copy code
```go
func TestAddTableDriven(t *testing.T) {
    tests := []struct {
        name     string
        a, b     int
        expected int
```

```go
}{
    {"positive numbers", 2, 3, 5},
    {"zero values", 0, 0, 0},
    {"negative numbers", -1, -1, -2},
}

for _, tt := range tests {
    t.Run(tt.name, func(t *testing.T) {
        result := Add(tt.a, tt.b)
        if result != tt.expected {
            t.Errorf("Add(%d, %d) = %d; want %d", tt.a, tt.b,
result, tt.expected)
        }
    })
}
}
```

Using t.Run, each subtest gets its own context, which helps
in identifying which test case failed.

4. Running the Tests

Command Line:
Run all tests in the current directory with:
bash

Copy code
go test

Verbose Output:

For more detailed output, use the -v flag:
bash
Copy code
go test -v

5. Best Practice

Isolate Test Cases:

Each unit test should focus on a single function or behavior, making it easier to pinpoint issues when tests fail.

Use Table-Driven Tests:

This approach helps manage multiple test scenarios in a concise and readable way.

Clean Up Resources:

If your tests allocate resources (files, network connections, etc.), use t.Cleanup or defer statements to ensure resources are released properly after the test runs.

Consistent Test Naming:

Descriptive test function names and subtest names make your tests self-documenting and easier to maintain.

Conclusion

The testing package in Go is a robust and straightforward tool for writing unit tests. By following conventions—such as naming test files with _test.go, writing functions that start with Test, and adopting table-driven tests—you can create a comprehensive suite of tests that improve code quality and maintainability. Whether you're testing simple functions or more complex interactions, Go's testing framework provides the flexibility and clarity needed to build reliable applications.

5.2 Benchmarking Your Code

Benchmarking in Go is a vital practice for measuring and optimizing the performance of your code. Go's testing framework provides built-in support for benchmarks, allowing you to write functions that measure how long particular code segments take to execute. Here's an overview of how to benchmark your code in Go:

1. Benchmark Function Structure
Benchmark functions are similar to test functions but must start with Benchmark and accept a single parameter of type *testing.B. The standard structure of a benchmark function is as follows:

```go
Copy code
func BenchmarkMyFunction(b *testing.B) {
    for i := 0; i < b.N; i++ {
        // Code you want to benchmark
        MyFunction()
    }
}
```

b.N: The benchmarking tool controls the number of iterations (b.N) to achieve reliable timing results. The framework adjusts this count automatically to provide accurate measurements.

Loop Structure: All the code you want to measure should be inside the loop that iterates b.N times. This ensures that the benchmark reflects the function's performance under repeated use.

2. Writing a Simple Benchmark

Suppose you have a function that performs a simple computation:

```go
Copy code
// File: compute.go
package compute

func Sum(a, b int) int {
    return a + b
}
```

You can create a benchmark for the Sum function like this:

go
Copy code
```go
// File: compute_test.go
package compute

import "testing"

func BenchmarkSum(b *testing.B) {
  for i := 0; i < b.N; i++ {
    Sum(2, 3)
  }
}
```

Running go test -bench=. will execute the benchmark and report the average time per operation.

3. Benchmarking Best Practices

Isolate the Code to Benchmark:

Ensure that the code inside your benchmark loop is minimal and represents the functionality you want to measure. Avoid including setup or teardown code inside the loop; if necessary, perform those operations outside or use b.ResetTimer() to exclude their time.

Use b.ResetTimer():

If your benchmark function includes initialization that you don't want to measure, call b.ResetTimer() right before entering the main loop. This resets the elapsed benchmark timer.

```go
Copy code
func BenchmarkComplexOperation(b *testing.B) {
    setupData := prepareData() // Setup outside the measured code
    b.ResetTimer()
    for i := 0; i < b.N; i++ {
        ComplexOperation(setupData)
    }
}
```

Avoid Unnecessary Memory Allocations:

Benchmark functions can also track memory allocations by calling b.ReportAllocs(). This is useful if you want to ensure that your code is not only fast but also memory efficient.

```go
Copy code
func BenchmarkSum(b *testing.B) {
    b.ReportAllocs()
    for i := 0; i < b.N; i++ {
        Sum(2, 3)
    }
}
```

Run Benchmarks in Isolation:

Benchmarks can be influenced by external factors like CPU load. For more consistent results, run them on a dedicated system or use benchmarking flags like -cpu to specify the number of CPU cores used.

4. Analyzing Benchmark Results

When you run benchmarks using:

bash

Copy code

```
go test -bench=.
```

You'll see output similar to:

bash
Copy code

```
BenchmarkSum-8      2000000000      0.30 ns/op      0 B/op      0 allocs/op
```

ns/op: Average time taken per operation.

B/op: Average number of bytes allocated per operation.

allocs/op: Average number of allocations per operation.

BenchmarkSum-8: Indicates the benchmark name and the number of CPU cores used.

Conclusion

Benchmarking your code in Go is straightforward with the built-in support provided by the testing package. By writing benchmark functions, isolating the code under test, and using best practices like resetting timers and reporting allocations, you can gain valuable insights into the performance characteristics of your code. These insights help you identify bottlenecks and optimize your functions, ultimately leading to more efficient and performant applications.

5.3 Debugging Techniques and Tools

Debugging is an essential aspect of software development, and Go provides a variety of techniques and tools to help you diagnose and fix issues in your code efficiently. Below are several strategies and tools commonly used for debugging Go applications:

1. Print Debugging and Logging

Print Statements:

One of the simplest debugging methods is inserting print statements (e.g., using fmt.Println or log.Printf) to inspect variable values and track the flow of execution. Although straightforward, this technique can be effective for quickly identifying issues in small sections of code.

Structured Logging:

Leveraging logging libraries (such as Go's built-in log package or third-party libraries like logrus or zap) can help create more organized, level-based logs (info, warning, error, etc.). Structured logs are especially useful in production environments where analyzing logs is crucial for diagnosing problems.

2. Delve Debugger

What is Delve?

Delve is a powerful, open-source debugger for Go. It allows you to set breakpoints, step through code line by line, inspect variables, and evaluate expressions in real time.

Using Delve:
You can run your Go application under Delve's control by invoking:

```bash
Copy code
dlv debug
```

or attach to a running process:

```bash
Copy code
dlv attach <pid>
```

Integrated development environments (IDEs) like Visual Studio Code (with the Go extension) and GoLand provide built-in support for Delve, offering a graphical interface for an enhanced debugging experience.

3. Race Detector

Detecting Concurrency Issues:

Go's race detector is a built-in tool that identifies race conditions in concurrent code. Run your tests or application with the -race flag:

```bash
Copy code
go run -race main.go
go test -race ./...
```

The race detector instruments your program to catch concurrent access issues, which can be notoriously difficult to debug manually.

4. Static Analysis Tools

go vet:
This tool examines your source code and reports suspicious constructs, potential bugs, and code patterns that may not be idiomatic or safe. Running go vet is a good practice as it often catches issues that might not trigger a runtime error.

Linters:

Tools like golint and staticcheck provide additional static analysis, flagging potential errors, style issues, and performance improvements. Integrating these tools into your development workflow can prevent many common mistakes before they become bugs.

5. Profiling and Tracing
pprof:

While primarily used for performance profiling, the pprof tool can also help identify unexpected behavior, such as memory leaks or CPU-intensive operations. By capturing and analyzing profiles, you can gain insights into the runtime behavior of your application.

Runtime Tracing:

The runtime/trace package allows you to record a detailed trace of your program's execution, which can be invaluable for understanding complex interactions, especially in concurrent programs.

6. Best Practices for Effective Debugging
Reproduce Issues Consistently:

Try to isolate and reproduce bugs in a controlled environment. Writing small test cases or using minimal examples can help pinpoint the problem more quickly.

Use Version Control:

Regularly commit changes and use version control tools to compare different versions of your code. This can help identify when and where a bug was introduced.

Test-Driven Development (TDD):

Writing tests that expose bugs can be an effective way to ensure that fixes work and that regressions do not reappear in the future.

Documentation and Comments:

Document the intended behavior of your code. Clear comments and documentation can make it easier for you and others to understand why a particular piece of code exists, which in turn can simplify the debugging process.

Conclusion

Effective debugging in Go combines traditional techniques like print statements and logging with more advanced tools such as Delve, the race detector, and static analysis utilities. By integrating these strategies into your development workflow, you can systematically identify and resolve issues, ultimately leading to more robust, efficient, and maintainable code.

5.4 Profiling Go Applications

Profiling Go applications is essential for understanding performance characteristics, identifying bottlenecks, and optimizing resource usage. Go includes robust built-in tools that help developers measure and analyze how their code executes, particularly in CPU usage, memory allocation, and concurrency behavior.

1. The Role of Profiling

Profiling is the process of collecting data about an application's runtime behavior. This data helps you answer questions such as:

Which parts of the code consume the most CPU time?
Where are the most memory allocations occurring?
Are there any memory leaks or unnecessary resource usages?
How is the application performing under concurrent loads?
Profiling provides actionable insights that enable you to focus optimization efforts where they will have the greatest impact.

2. The pprof Tool

Go's net/http/pprof package and command-line tool pprof are the primary tools for profiling Go applications. They support several types of profiles:

CPU Profiling:

Captures which functions are consuming CPU time.

Memory Profiling:

Tracks memory allocations to detect excessive memory usage or leaks.

Block Profiling:

Identifies code that may be causing goroutines to block, such as waiting on locks.

Goroutine Profiling:

Provides a snapshot of all goroutines to help identify concurrency issues.

Example Usage:

To profile a running application, you can import the net/http/pprof package. For example, by adding the following code snippet to your main package, you can serve profiling data over HTTP:

```go
Copy code
import (
    _ "net/http/pprof"
    "log"
    "net/http"
)

func main() {
    // Start an HTTP server for pprof on a dedicated port
    go func() {
        log.Println(http.ListenAndServe("localhost:6060", nil))
    }()

    // Your application code goes here...
}
```

Then, you can access profiles by navigating to URLs such as http://localhost:6060/debug/pprof/ in your browser or by using the go tool pprof command-line utility.

Capturing a CPU Profile:

bash
Copy code

```
go test -cpuprofile=cpu.prof -bench=. ./...
```

Once captured, you can analyze the profile:

bash
Copy code

```
go tool pprof cpu.prof
```

Inside the interactive pprof tool, commands like top or list <function_name> help you inspect which functions are consuming the most resources.

3. Runtime Tracing

Beyond pprof, Go offers the runtime/trace package to generate detailed execution traces. These traces capture fine-grained events such as goroutine scheduling, system calls, and garbage collection pauses.

Generating a Trace:

```go
import (
    "os"
    "runtime/trace"
    "log"
)

func main() {
    f, err := os.Create("trace.out")
    if err != nil {
        log.Fatalf("failed to create trace output file: %v", err)
    }
    defer f.Close()

    if err := trace.Start(f); err != nil {
        log.Fatalf("failed to start trace: %v", err)
    }
    defer trace.Stop()

    // Your application code here
}
```

After running your application, analyze the trace using:

```bash
Copy code
go tool trace trace.out
```

This command opens a web-based interface where you can visually inspect the execution timeline, helping you identify performance issues related to concurrency and blocking.

4. Best Practices for Profiling
Profile in Realistic Conditions:

Ensure that profiling is done under conditions that resemble production as closely as possible. Synthetic benchmarks can be misleading if they don't reflect actual workloads.

Minimize Profiling Overhead:

Some profiling tools can introduce overhead. Use profiling judiciously and consider isolating the performance-critical sections of your code.

Analyze Multiple Profiles:

Collect and compare different profiles (CPU, memory, block, and goroutine) to get a comprehensive view of your application's performance.

Automate and Integrate:

Integrate profiling into your continuous integration workflow to catch performance regressions early.

Conclusion

Profiling is a powerful technique for uncovering performance issues in Go applications. Tools like pprof and runtime/trace provide deep insights into how your application consumes CPU and memory and how it manages concurrency. By regularly profiling your code, analyzing the resulting data, and applying targeted optimizations, you can ensure that your applications run efficiently and scale effectively under load.

Chapter 6
Optimizing Performance

Optimizing performance in Go involves a combination of writing efficient, idiomatic code and leveraging the language's built-in tools to identify and resolve bottlenecks. Here are some key considerations:

Understand the Go Runtime:

Familiarize yourself with Go's concurrency model, garbage collector, and scheduler. This knowledge helps you write code that minimizes unnecessary context switches and resource contention.

Efficient Memory Usage:

Minimize memory allocations by reusing objects and avoiding excessive copying. Use profiling tools like pprof to detect memory hotspots and optimize garbage collection performance.

Concurrency Best Practices:

Utilize goroutines and channels effectively to handle concurrent tasks, and apply synchronization primitives only when necessary. The Go race detector can help you catch concurrency issues that may impact performance.

Profiling and Benchmarking:

Regularly benchmark your code with the testing package's benchmarking functions and analyze performance using tools like go tool pprof and runtime/trace. This data-driven approach ensures that you focus optimization efforts where they matter most.

Optimize Algorithms and Data Structures:

Select appropriate algorithms and data structures that suit your workload. Simple, well-structured code often performs better than overly complex solutions.

By continuously profiling, measuring, and refining your code, you can identify performance bottlenecks and apply targeted improvements to ensure your Go applications run efficiently even under heavy load.

6.1 Understanding Go's Runtime

Understanding Go's runtime is key to writing efficient and scalable applications in Go. The runtime is the underlying layer that manages how your Go programs execute, handling aspects such as concurrency, memory management, and garbage collection. Here's an overview of its main components and their significance:

1. Goroutine Scheduling

Lightweight Concurrency:

Go uses goroutines—lightweight, user-space threads—to enable concurrent programming. Goroutines are much more efficient in terms of memory and scheduling overhead compared to traditional operating system threads.

Work Stealing Scheduler:

The runtime includes a scheduler that multiplexes thousands of goroutines onto a smaller number of OS threads. It employs a work stealing algorithm, ensuring that goroutines are balanced across available CPU cores. This design minimizes idle time and optimizes parallel execution.

Cooperative Scheduling:

Goroutines yield control voluntarily (for example, when performing blocking operations or using certain runtime functions), which allows the scheduler to interleave execution and maintain responsiveness.

2. Memory Management and Garbage Collection

Automatic Memory Management:

Go's runtime takes care of allocating and freeing memory through a garbage collector (GC). The GC runs concurrently with the program, reclaiming memory that is no longer reachable, thereby reducing the risk of memory leaks and segmentation faults.

Generational Improvements:

Over successive Go releases, the garbage collector has been optimized to reduce pause times and improve overall performance. Its concurrent, mark-and-sweep approach helps ensure that GC interruptions are minimal, even in applications with large heaps.

Efficient Allocation:

The runtime also manages a memory allocator optimized for the patterns common in Go programs. This allocator aims to minimize fragmentation and provides efficient allocation for both short-lived and long-lived objects.

3. Concurrency Primitives and Synchronization

Channels and Select:

Go's runtime supports channels, which are first-class primitives for communication between goroutines. The select statement further enhances this by allowing a goroutine to wait on multiple communication operations simultaneously.

Synchronization Tools:

In addition to channels, the runtime provides synchronization mechanisms such as mutexes, wait groups, and condition variables (found in the sync package). These tools help coordinate access to shared resources, ensuring thread safety in concurrent environments.

4. Profiling and Debugging Support
Built-in Instrumentation:

The runtime is designed to work seamlessly with profiling tools like pprof and tracing tools from the runtime/trace package. These tools provide insights into CPU usage, memory allocation, and goroutine behavior, enabling developers to fine-tune performance.

Race Detection:

Go's runtime includes a race detector that, when enabled with the -race flag, helps identify data races in concurrent code. This built-in feature is invaluable for ensuring the correctness of multithreaded applications.

5. Impact on Application Design

Optimizing for Concurrency:
A deep understanding of Go's runtime allows developers to design applications that make the best use of goroutines and channels, avoid unnecessary blocking, and prevent contention.

Balancing Performance and Safety:

While the runtime abstracts many low-level details, being aware of its behavior helps you avoid common pitfalls, such as excessive goroutine creation or unintentional memory pressure, which can degrade performance.

Fine-Tuning Garbage Collection:

Developers can sometimes influence GC behavior through proper allocation patterns and by configuring GC parameters. This can be especially useful in performance-critical applications where latency is a concern.

Conclusion

Go's runtime is a sophisticated component that manages concurrency, memory, and execution scheduling. By handling goroutines, garbage collection, and synchronization behind the scenes, the runtime enables developers to write concurrent and efficient code without getting bogged down by low-level details. Understanding these aspects not only helps in optimizing performance but also in writing more predictable and robust applications in Go.

6.2 Memory Optimization and Garbage Collection

Memory optimization and garbage collection are critical factors in achieving high-performance Go applications. Efficient memory usage can lower latency and reduce resource consumption, while a well-tuned garbage collector (GC) ensures that memory is reclaimed promptly without impacting overall performance. Below, we explore techniques for memory optimization in Go and how its garbage collection mechanism works.

Memory Optimization Techniques
Minimize Allocations:

Reuse Objects:

Whenever possible, reuse memory rather than allocating new objects. Go's sync.Pool is designed for this purpose by providing a temporary object cache that can reduce allocation overhead in high-frequency code paths.

Avoid Unnecessary Copies:

Use pointers judiciously to avoid copying large structures. However, balance this with the cost of dereferencing and the clarity of your code.

Efficient Data Structures:

Choose data structures that match your workload. For instance, slices are typically more efficient than arrays when dealing with dynamic data sizes, and maps should be sized appropriately to avoid frequent resizing.

Optimize Allocation Patterns:

Preallocate Slices:

If you know the approximate size of a slice in advance, preallocate it to the needed capacity. This avoids repeated allocations and copying as the slice grows.

Escape Analysis Awareness:

Understand how the compiler's escape analysis works—variables that "escape" to the heap incur allocation overhead. Writing functions and structuring code to minimize escapes can keep more data on the stack, which is faster to allocate and deallocate.

Profile and Measure:

Use Profiling Tools:

Tools like pprof help you identify allocation hotspots and memory leaks. By analyzing heap profiles, you can pinpoint functions or sections of code responsible for excessive memory usage.

Benchmarking:

Combine benchmarks with memory allocation reporting (using b.ReportAllocs()) to track the impact of optimizations on both speed and memory consumption.

Garbage Collection in Go

Garbage Collector Overview:

Automatic Memory Reclamation:

Go's garbage collector is designed to automatically reclaim memory that is no longer in use. It uses a concurrent, tri-color mark-and-sweep algorithm that runs alongside your application, minimizing stop-the-world pauses.

Concurrent Collection:

Modern versions of Go feature a concurrent GC, which aims to reduce pause times by spreading out work over the application's lifetime. This ensures that even applications with large heaps can remain responsive.

Tuning the Garbage Collector:

GOGC Environment Variable:

The GOGC variable controls the aggressiveness of the garbage collector. A lower GOGC value causes the GC to run more frequently, potentially reducing peak memory usage at the expense of increased CPU overhead, whereas a higher value defers collection for longer periods.

Monitoring GC Impact:

Use runtime metrics and profiling tools to monitor GC behavior. Metrics such as pause times, GC cycles, and heap sizes can help you understand how the GC impacts your application's performance.

Balancing Performance and Memory Efficiency:

Trade-Offs:

Memory optimization and garbage collection tuning often involve trade-offs between throughput and latency. Aggressive GC tuning may reduce memory footprint but can introduce more frequent pauses, while a more lenient GC may improve throughput but at the cost of higher memory consumption.

Application-Specific Considerations:

The optimal balance depends on your application's workload. For latency-sensitive applications, minimizing pause times is crucial, while for batch processing tasks, overall throughput might be the priority.

Conclusion

Optimizing memory usage in Go is a continuous process that involves writing allocation-efficient code and leveraging profiling tools to identify and address memory hotspots. At the same time, understanding and tuning Go's garbage collector—through mechanisms like the GOGC variable and concurrent GC profiling—can help ensure that your application remains responsive and efficient even under heavy loads. By combining these techniques, you can build

Go applications that perform well in both memory-constrained and high-performance environments.

6.3 Reducing Latency and Improving Throughput

Reducing latency and improving throughput are key performance objectives in modern Go applications, especially in high-concurrency or real-time environments. Both goals focus on optimizing the responsiveness of your system and its ability to handle a high volume of work efficiently. Here are several strategies and considerations for achieving these objectives:

1. Efficient Concurrency and Scheduling

Leverage Goroutines:

Go's lightweight goroutines enable massive concurrency with minimal overhead. Design your application to perform work concurrently, thereby reducing the time each request waits to be processed.

Optimized Scheduling:

The built-in scheduler in Go efficiently multiplexes goroutines onto OS threads. Minimize long-running or blocking operations within goroutines to avoid stalling the scheduler.

Minimize Lock Contention:

Use channels or fine-grained locking to reduce bottlenecks. When locks are necessary, design your critical sections to be as short as possible to prevent delays in processing.

2. Asynchronous and Non-Blocking I/O

Non-Blocking Operations:

Reduce latency by handling I/O-bound tasks asynchronously. Use Go's support for asynchronous network and file operations so that goroutines do not block while waiting for I/O.

Batching and Pipelining:

When possible, batch multiple operations together or implement pipelining techniques. This reduces overhead by amortizing costs over multiple requests or data items.

3. Memory Optimization and Garbage

Collection Tuning

Reduce Allocation Overhead:

Frequent memory allocations can lead to increased garbage collection (GC) activity, which in turn can cause latency spikes. Use techniques such as object pooling (sync.Pool) and preallocating slices to minimize dynamic memory allocation.

Tune the Garbage Collector:

Adjust the GOGC setting to balance between memory usage and GC pause times. For latency-sensitive applications, a lower GOGC value may trigger more frequent collections with shorter pause durations, while a higher value can improve throughput at the risk of longer GC pauses.

4. Algorithmic and Data Structure Optimization

Choose Efficient Algorithms:

Optimize computational paths by selecting algorithms with lower time complexity. Even small improvements in an algorithm can have a significant impact on overall latency and throughput.

Optimize Data Structures:

Use data structures that are tailored to your workload. For example, using a slice with preallocated capacity or a concurrent map optimized for low contention can reduce overhead and speed up data access.

5. Profiling and Continuous Improvement
Profile Regularly:

Use Go's profiling tools such as pprof and runtime/trace to identify hotspots, measure GC behavior, and monitor CPU/memory usage. This data is essential for making informed optimizations.

Benchmark and Test Changes:

Employ benchmarks to validate the performance improvements of your optimizations. Tools in the testing package, like b.ReportAllocs(), help quantify both speed and memory allocation impacts.

6. System-Level Optimizations

Load Balancing and Caching:

Distribute workload efficiently across multiple cores or servers. Implement caching strategies to serve frequently requested data faster and reduce processing load.

Network and I/O Tuning:

Optimize network configurations and utilize faster storage options where possible. Low-latency network libraries or tuning TCP parameters can also contribute to reducing overall latency.

Conclusion

Reducing latency and improving throughput in Go applications is a multifaceted challenge that involves optimizing code-level constructs, efficient use of Go's concurrency model, minimizing memory allocation overhead, and fine-tuning system-level configurations. By carefully profiling your application and iteratively applying these techniques, you can achieve a responsive system that scales efficiently under heavy loads.

6.4 Using pprof for Performance Analysis

pprof is a powerful tool built into Go that enables developers to perform detailed performance analysis of their applications. By generating and analyzing profiles, you can identify CPU bottlenecks, excessive memory allocations, and inefficient code paths. Here's how you can use pprof for performance analysis:

1. Generating Profiles

CPU Profiling:

To capture a CPU profile, you can either use Go's built-in testing support or manually trigger profiling in your application code.

Via Testing:

When writing benchmarks or tests, you can generate a CPU profile with:

```bash
Copy code
go test -bench=. -cpuprofile=cpu.prof ./...
```

This command runs your benchmarks and writes the CPU profile data to cpu.prof.

Programmatically:

In your application, import the runtime/pprof package and start profiling:

```go
Copy code
import (
    "os"
    "runtime/pprof"
```

```go
    "log"
)

func main() {
    f, err := os.Create("cpu.prof")
    if err != nil {
        log.Fatal(err)
    }
    defer f.Close()

    if err := pprof.StartCPUProfile(f); err != nil {
        log.Fatal(err)
    }
    defer pprof.StopCPUProfile()

    // Your application logic here
}
```

Memory Profiling:

Memory profiles are useful for identifying where allocations occur. To capture a memory profile, you can write:

go
Copy code

```go
import (
    "os"
    "runtime/pprof"
    "log"
)

func main() {
    // Application logic here

    f, err := os.Create("mem.prof")
    if err != nil {
        log.Fatal(err)
    }
    defer f.Close()

    // Write a heap profile.
    if err := pprof.WriteHeapProfile(f); err != nil {
        log.Fatal(err)
    }
}
```

2. Analyzing Profiles with pprof

Once you have generated a profile (e.g., cpu.prof or mem.prof), use the go tool pprof command to analyze it:

Interactive Command-Line Interface:

Run the following command to start an interactive session:

bash
Copy code
go tool pprof cpu.prof

Within the interactive prompt, common commands include:

top: Displays the functions that consumed the most CPU time.
list <function_name>: Shows the source code annotated with CPU usage for a specific function.
web: Opens an SVG visualization in your browser for a graphical call graph.
help: Lists available commands.

Web-Based Interface:

You can also generate an interactive web interface directly:

bash
Copy code

```
go tool pprof -http=":8080" cpu.prof
```

Navigating to http://localhost:8080 in your browser will display detailed graphs and tables that help visualize hotspots and call relationships.

3. Best Practices for Using pprof

Profile in Realistic Conditions:

Run your application under workloads that closely mimic production. Synthetic benchmarks are useful, but real-world usage data provides more actionable insights.

Focus on Hotspots:

Use the data from pprof to focus your optimization efforts on the parts of the code that consume the most resources. Even small improvements in hotspot areas can have a significant impact on overall performance.

Iterate and Reprofile:

Performance optimization is iterative. After making changes, re-run your profiles to verify that the adjustments have led to improvements without introducing new issues.

Combine with Other Tools:

While pprof is excellent for CPU and memory profiling, consider using additional tools like runtime/trace for deeper insights into goroutine scheduling and blocking behavior, or the race detector (go run -race) to identify concurrency issues.

Conclusion

Using pprof for performance analysis in Go is a highly effective way to understand the runtime behavior of your applications. By generating CPU and memory profiles and analyzing them through both command-line and web interfaces, you can pinpoint inefficiencies and optimize critical code paths. This iterative process of profiling, analyzing, and optimizing helps ensure that your Go applications run efficiently, even under heavy loads.

Part III: Concurrency and Scalability

.

Chapter 7
Concurrency in Go

Concurrency in Go is built into the language and is one of its defining features. Go's approach to concurrency is centered around two primary constructs:

Goroutines:

Goroutines are lightweight functions that run concurrently. They are inexpensive to create and managed by Go's runtime scheduler, allowing thousands of them to run concurrently without significant overhead.

Channels:

Channels provide a way for goroutines to communicate safely and synchronize by passing messages. This message-passing paradigm encourages designing programs that avoid shared memory, reducing the risk of race conditions.

Together, goroutines and channels enable developers to write concurrent programs in a clear and manageable way. Additionally, Go provides synchronization tools in the sync package and a race detector to help catch concurrency-related issues, ensuring that applications are both performant and reliable.

7.1 Goroutines: Lightweight Threads

Goroutines are one of Go's most powerful features, enabling concurrent execution of functions in a highly efficient manner. They are often described as "lightweight threads" because they have a much lower overhead than traditional operating system threads. Here are some key aspects of goroutines:

1. Easy to Launch

Syntax:

Starting a new goroutine is as simple as prefixing a function call with the go keyword:

```go
Copy code
go doWork()
```

This spawns a new goroutine that executes doWork() concurrently with the rest of the program.

Minimal Overhead:

Goroutines are designed to be lightweight. While an OS thread might consume megabytes of memory, a goroutine typically starts with a small stack (often just a few kilobytes) that grows and shrinks dynamically as needed.

2. Managed by the Go Runtime Scheduler

Concurrency Model:

The Go runtime includes a scheduler that efficiently manages thousands (or even millions) of goroutines across a smaller number of OS threads. This scheduler uses techniques like work-stealing to balance the load, ensuring that available CPU resources are utilized effectively.

Non-Blocking Nature:

When a goroutine performs a blocking operation (such as waiting for I/O), the scheduler automatically suspends it and switches to another runnable goroutine. This helps maintain high levels of concurrency without wasting resources.

3. Communication and Synchronization

Inter-Goroutine Communication:

Goroutines often communicate using channels, which provide a safe and structured way to pass data between concurrent processes. Channels help to avoid explicit locking and shared memory issues:

```go
Copy code
ch := make(chan int)
go func() {
   ch <- 42
}()
value := <-ch
```

Coordination Tools:

In addition to channels, Go provides synchronization primitives in the sync package (e.g., mutexes, wait groups) to coordinate goroutines when necessary.

4. Advantages of Goroutines

Scalability:

Because they are so lightweight, you can spawn thousands of goroutines to perform tasks concurrently. This makes them ideal for building highly concurrent systems, such as web servers or real-time data processors.

Simplified Concurrency:

The use of goroutines and channels abstracts much of the complexity involved in traditional concurrent programming. Developers can focus on the logic of their applications rather than the intricacies of thread management and synchronization.

Improved Resource Utilization:

Goroutines allow your application to make full use of multi-core processors by efficiently managing concurrent execution, which can lead to significant improvements in throughput and responsiveness.

Conclusion

Goroutines are a fundamental component of Go's concurrency model. Their ease of use, low memory footprint, and efficient scheduling enable developers to write concurrent applications that are both scalable and performant. By combining goroutines with channels and other synchronization tools, you can create robust, concurrent systems with relatively simple and maintainable code.

7.2 Channels: Communicating Between Goroutines

Channels are a core feature in Go that facilitate safe and efficient communication between goroutines. They allow you to pass data from one goroutine to another without relying on shared memory, thereby reducing the risk of race conditions and other concurrency issues. Below are some key points about channels and how they enable communication between goroutines:

1. Creating and Declaring Channels
Declaration:

A channel in Go is a typed conduit through which you can send and receive values. The syntax for declaring a channel that carries values of type T is:

```go
Copy code
var ch chan T
```

For example, to declare a channel for integers:

```go
Copy code
var intCh chan int
```

Initialization:

Channels must be created with the make function before use:

go
Copy code
```go
intCh := make(chan int)
```

You can also create buffered channels by specifying a capacity:

go
Copy code
```go
bufferedCh := make(chan int, 10)
```

Buffered channels allow a limited number of values to be sent without requiring an immediate receiver.

2. Sending and Receiving Data

Sending Data:

To send a value to a channel, use the <- operator:

go
Copy code
```go
intCh <- 42
```

This operation will block until another goroutine is ready to receive the value, unless the channel is buffered and has available capacity.

Receiving Data:
To receive a value from a channel, you also use the <- operator:

```go
Copy code
value := <-intCh
```

This operation will block until a value is available if the channel is empty.

Bidirectional Communication:

Channels naturally support bidirectional communication, meaning you can both send to and receive from the same channel. However, you can restrict channels to only sending or receiving in function parameters for clarity:

```go
Copy code
func send(ch chan<- int, value int) {
    ch <- value
```

```go
}

func receive(ch <-chan int) int {
    return <-ch
}
```

3. Synchronization Through Channels

Implicit Synchronization:

The blocking behavior of channels means that they inherently synchronize the execution of goroutines. For example, in an unbuffered channel, a send operation will block until another goroutine performs a corresponding receive, ensuring that the data exchange occurs in a coordinated manner.

Signaling Completion:

Channels can also be used as signals. For example, you can send a special value or close a channel to indicate that no more data will be sent:

```go
Copy code
```

```
close(intCh)
```

After a channel is closed, receivers can still retrieve any buffered values, and subsequent receive operations yield the zero value of the channel's type along with a boolean value indicating that the channel is closed.

4. The select Statement

Multiple Channel Operations:

The select statement in Go provides a way to wait on multiple channel operations. It allows a goroutine to proceed with the first channel that is ready:

```go
Copy code
select {
case msg := <-ch1:
    fmt.Println("Received from ch1:", msg)
case ch2 <- 100:
    fmt.Println("Sent to ch2")
default:
    fmt.Println("No channel ready")
}
```

Using select makes it easier to manage complex concurrent workflows where multiple channels are involved.

5. Benefits of Using Channels

Safe Communication:

Channels provide a safe and structured way for goroutines to communicate without sharing memory directly. This aligns with the Go philosophy of "don't communicate by sharing memory; share memory by communicating."

Simplified Concurrency:

With channels, you can coordinate goroutines in a natural way. Instead of managing locks and other synchronization primitives, you can use channels to signal events, pass data, and synchronize tasks.

Readability and Maintainability:

Code that uses channels often reflects the logical flow of concurrent operations, making it easier to understand how data moves through the system and how different parts of the program interact.

Conclusion

Channels are a powerful feature in Go that enable safe, efficient communication and synchronization between goroutines. By leveraging channels, you can design concurrent systems that are both robust and easy to reason about. Whether using unbuffered channels for synchronous communication or buffered channels for asynchronous operations, channels play a crucial role in managing concurrency in Go applications.

7.3 Select Statements and Patterns

The select statement in Go is a powerful control structure designed to handle multiple channel operations concurrently. It allows a goroutine to wait on several communication operations and proceed with the one that's ready first. This mechanism not only simplifies concurrent programming but also provides a flexible way to implement various communication patterns. Here's an overview of select statements and common patterns associated with them:

1. Basic Syntax and Behavior

Syntax Overview:

A select statement is similar to a switch statement but is specialized for channel operations. Its basic form is:

```go
Copy code
select {
case msg1 := <-ch1:
    // Handle message received from ch1.
case ch2 <- msg2:
    // Handle sending msg2 to ch2.
default:
    // Optional default case executed if no channel is ready.
}
```

Blocking and Non-Blocking Behavior:

If one or more of the channel operations (send or receive) are ready, the select chooses one at random and executes its corresponding case.

If none of the channels are ready and there is no default case, the select statement blocks until one becomes available. Including a default case makes the select non-blocking—if no channel is ready, the default case executes immediately.

2. Common Patterns Using select

Multiplexing Channel Operations:

The most common use of select is to listen on multiple channels simultaneously. For example, if you have several channels from which data might arrive, you can handle the first one that's ready:

```go
Copy code
select {
case msg := <-ch1:
    fmt.Println("Received from ch1:", msg)
case msg := <-ch2:
    fmt.Println("Received from ch2:", msg)
}
```

Implementing Timeouts:

You can use the time.After function within a select to implement a timeout for channel operations. This pattern is especially useful when you want to avoid indefinite blocking:

```go
Copy code
select {
case msg := <-ch:
    fmt.Println("Received message:", msg)
case <-time.After(2 * time.Second):
        fmt.Println("Timeout: no message received within 2 seconds")
}
```

Non-Blocking Channel Operations:

When you want to attempt a channel operation without waiting, you can include a default case:

```go
Copy code
select {
case msg := <-ch:
    fmt.Println("Received message:", msg)
```

```
default:
    fmt.Println("No message available; moving on")
}
```

Fan-In Pattern:

Combining multiple channels into a single channel output can be implemented using a select inside a loop. This pattern, known as "fan-in," is useful when you need to consolidate results from several concurrent goroutines:

```go
Copy code
for i := 0; i < numChannels; i++ {
    select {
    case msg := <-ch1:
        process(msg)
    case msg := <-ch2:
        process(msg)
    // Additional cases can be added as needed.
    }
}
```

Fan-Out Pattern:

Conversely, you can use select within multiple goroutines to distribute work (fan-out) and then use a channel to collect results. Although the fan-out pattern often involves spawning several goroutines, the select statement can be used within each to manage multiple incoming signals or cancellation requests.

3. Advanced Considerations

Randomized Selection:

When multiple cases in a select are ready simultaneously, Go picks one at random. This randomness can help distribute work evenly but should be kept in mind if order or fairness is a requirement.

Combining with Context:

In real-world applications, you might use a select to handle context cancellation along with channel operations. For example:

```go
Copy code
select {
```

```
case msg := <-ch:
   fmt.Println("Received message:", msg)
case <-ctx.Done():
   fmt.Println("Operation canceled")
}
```

This pattern allows you to gracefully handle cancellation signals in long-running operations.

Error and Signal Handling:

select can also be used to listen for system signals (using channels provided by the os/signal package) alongside other channel communications, enabling clean shutdown procedures.

Conclusion

The select statement is a versatile tool in Go's concurrency toolkit. By enabling a goroutine to wait on multiple channel operations, it simplifies handling asynchronous events, implementing timeouts, and coordinating complex workflows. Understanding and mastering common patterns—such as multiplexing, fan-in/fan-out, and non-blocking operations—will help you write robust and responsive concurrent programs in Go.

7.4 Synchronization with sync Package

The sync package in Go provides a collection of synchronization primitives that make it easier to coordinate the execution of concurrent goroutines and manage access to shared resources. These tools help prevent race conditions, ensure data consistency, and simplify the design of concurrent algorithms. Below are some of the key components of the sync package and how they are typically used:

1. Mutexes

Purpose:

A Mutex (mutual exclusion lock) is used to protect shared data from being accessed concurrently. It allows only one goroutine to access a critical section of code at a time.

Basic Usage:

```go
Copy code
import (
    "fmt"
    "sync"
)

var (
    counter int
    mu      sync.Mutex
)

func increment() {
    mu.Lock()      // Acquire the lock
    counter++      // Critical section
    mu.Unlock()    // Release the lock
}

func main() {
    var wg sync.WaitGroup
    for i := 0; i < 1000; i++ {
        wg.Add(1)
        go func() {
```

```go
        defer wg.Done()
        increment()
    }()
}
wg.Wait()
fmt.Println("Counter:", counter)
}
```

In this example, the mu.Lock() and mu.Unlock() calls ensure that only one goroutine can increment the shared counter at any given time.

Read/Write Mutexes:

For cases where multiple goroutines need to read shared data concurrently, but writes must be exclusive, Go provides the sync.RWMutex. This allows multiple readers or one writer:

```go
go
Copy code
var rwmu sync.RWMutex
var data int

// Reading
```

```go
func readData() int {
    rwmu.RLock()       // Acquire read lock
    defer rwmu.RUnlock() // Release read lock
    return data
}

// Writing
func writeData(val int) {
    rwmu.Lock()        // Acquire write lock
    data = val
    rwmu.Unlock()       // Release write lock
}
```

2. WaitGroup

Purpose:

A WaitGroup is used to wait for a collection of goroutines to finish executing. It provides a simple way to synchronize the end of concurrent operations.

Basic Usage:

go
Copy code

```go
var wg sync.WaitGroup

func worker(id int) {
    defer wg.Done() // Signal that this goroutine is done
    fmt.Printf("Worker %d starting\n", id)
    // Simulate work
    fmt.Printf("Worker %d done\n", id)
}

func main() {
    for i := 1; i <= 5; i++ {
        wg.Add(1)   // Increment the WaitGroup counter
        go worker(i)
    }
    wg.Wait()        // Block until the WaitGroup counter is
zero
    fmt.Println("All workers completed")
}
```

3. Once

Purpose:

The Once type ensures that a piece of code is executed only once, even if called from multiple goroutines. This is particularly useful for one-time initialization.

Basic Usage:

```go
Copy code
var once sync.Once

func initialize() {
    fmt.Println("Initialization code runs only once")
}

func doSomething() {
    once.Do(initialize)  // initialize() will be executed only on the first call
    fmt.Println("Doing something")
}
```

4. Condition Variables (Cond)

Purpose:

A Cond variable is used to coordinate goroutines that need to wait for or announce changes in state. It is often paired with a Mutex to protect the condition being waited on.

Basic Usage:

```go
Copy code
var (
    mu    sync.Mutex
    cond  = sync.NewCond(&mu)
    ready bool
)

func waitForCondition() {
    mu.Lock()
    for !ready {      // Use a loop to avoid spurious wakeups
        cond.Wait()    // Wait releases the lock and suspends the
goroutine
    }
    fmt.Println("Condition met, proceeding...")
    mu.Unlock()
}

func signalCondition() {
    mu.Lock()
    ready = true
    cond.Broadcast()   // Wake up all waiting goroutines
    mu.Unlock()
```

```
}
```

Conclusion

The sync package is a cornerstone for writing concurrent Go programs. By using primitives such as Mutex and RWMutex for mutual exclusion, WaitGroup for orchestrating goroutine completion, Once for one-time initialization, and Cond for more advanced coordination, developers can manage concurrency effectively and build robust, race-free applications. Understanding and applying these tools is essential for ensuring that concurrent operations are performed safely and efficiently in Go.

Chapter 8
Advanced Concurrency Patterns

Advanced concurrency patterns in Go build on the basic primitives of goroutines and channels to address more complex coordination and performance challenges. Here are some key patterns:

Worker Pools:

A worker pool limits concurrency by creating a fixed number of worker goroutines that pull tasks from a shared channel. This pattern is useful for managing resources and controlling parallelism in CPU-bound or I/O-bound workloads.

Fan-In and Fan-Out:

Fan-Out: Distributes work across multiple goroutines that process tasks concurrently.
Fan-In: Aggregates results from several goroutines into a single channel, making it easier to manage outputs from parallel operations.

Pipeline Pattern:

Data flows through multiple stages where each stage is a goroutine, and channels connect the stages. This pattern streamlines complex processing tasks by breaking them into sequential, concurrent steps.

Context for Cancellation and Timeouts:

The context package enables coordinated cancellation and timeout management across multiple goroutines. It helps ensure that long-running operations can be gracefully stopped when no longer needed.

Semaphore and Rate Limiting:

Buffered channels can serve as semaphores to limit the number of concurrent operations, effectively controlling access to scarce resources and implementing rate limiting.

Error Grouping:

The errgroup package (from golang.org/x/sync/errgroup) allows you to run multiple goroutines concurrently while collecting and propagating errors, ensuring that a failure in one part of the concurrent process can cancel or signal issues across others.

These advanced patterns help structure concurrent programs to be more efficient, resilient, and maintainable, especially as the complexity of parallel tasks grows.

8.1 Worker Pools

Worker pools are a popular concurrency pattern in Go that help manage and limit the number of goroutines processing tasks concurrently. Instead of spawning a new goroutine for every task—which can lead to resource exhaustion—worker pools allow you to create a fixed number of worker goroutines that continuously receive and process jobs from a shared channel. This pattern is especially useful when dealing with a large volume of tasks or when you need to control resource usage tightly.

Key Concepts

Job Queue:

A channel that holds the tasks (jobs) to be processed. Workers read from this channel to retrieve new tasks.

Fixed Number of Workers:

Instead of dynamically creating goroutines for every task, you predefine a set number of worker goroutines that continuously process jobs from the job queue.

Synchronization:

Using synchronization primitives like sync.WaitGroup ensures that the main program waits until all jobs have been processed before exiting.

How Worker Pools Work

Job Producer:

A part of your program enqueues jobs into a channel. Jobs can be any unit of work, such as processing a file, handling a network request, or computing a result.

Worker Goroutines:

A fixed number of worker goroutines are started. Each worker listens on the job channel in a loop. When a job is available, a worker retrieves and processes it.

Graceful Shutdown:

Once all jobs are enqueued, the job channel is closed. Workers detect the closed channel and exit their loop, allowing the program to synchronize on their completion (commonly using a sync.WaitGroup).

Example Implementation

Below is a simplified example that illustrates a worker pool in Go:

```go
Copy code
package main

import (
    "fmt"
```

```go
    "sync"
    "time"
)

// Job represents a unit of work.
type Job struct {
    ID int
}

// worker is a function that processes jobs from the jobs
channel.
func worker(id int, jobs <-chan Job, wg *sync.WaitGroup) {
    defer wg.Done()
    for job := range jobs {
        // Simulate work by sleeping.
        fmt.Printf("Worker %d started job %d\n", id, job.ID)
        time.Sleep(time.Millisecond * 500)
        fmt.Printf("Worker %d finished job %d\n", id, job.ID)
    }
}

func main() {
    const numWorkers = 3
    const numJobs = 10
```

```go
// Create a buffered channel to hold jobs.
jobs := make(chan Job, numJobs)
var wg sync.WaitGroup

// Start worker goroutines.
for w := 1; w <= numWorkers; w++ {
  wg.Add(1)
  go worker(w, jobs, &wg)
}

// Send jobs to the workers.
for j := 1; j <= numJobs; j++ {
  jobs <- Job{ID: j}
}
close(jobs) // No more jobs will be sent.

// Wait for all workers to finish.
wg.Wait()
fmt.Println("All jobs processed")
}
```

Benefits of Using Worker Pools

Resource Control:

By limiting the number of workers, you prevent your application from creating too many goroutines, which can help manage CPU and memory usage effectively.

Improved Throughput:

Workers can be tuned to the optimal number based on your system's capabilities, ensuring a balanced load and efficient processing.

Simplified Error Handling:

With a controlled number of workers, managing errors or implementing retry logic becomes more straightforward.

Scalability:

Worker pools can easily be scaled up or down by adjusting the number of worker goroutines, making the pattern adaptable to different workload requirements.

Conclusion

Worker pools in Go are an effective way to manage concurrent task processing by limiting the number of active goroutines and organizing work through a job queue. This pattern not only helps in achieving better resource utilization and throughput but also simplifies error handling and system scalability. By using synchronization primitives like channels and sync.WaitGroup, you can build robust and efficient concurrent systems that are easier to maintain and scale.

8.2 Fan-In and Fan-Out Patterns

Fan-In and Fan-Out are complementary concurrency patterns in Go that help manage and organize work across multiple goroutines. They are particularly useful when you need to distribute tasks among several workers (Fan-Out) and then collect or merge their results into a single channel (Fan-In).

Fan-Out Pattern
Purpose:

The Fan-Out pattern distributes work from a single source to multiple goroutines. This allows parallel processing of tasks, which can improve throughput and reduce latency.

How It Works:

A single producer sends tasks (or data) to a channel.
Multiple worker goroutines, often organized as a worker pool, receive tasks from the shared channel concurrently.
Each worker processes its assigned task independently.

Example:

```go
Copy code
func worker(id int, jobs <-chan int, results chan<- int) {
    for j := range jobs {
        fmt.Printf("Worker %d processing job %d\n", id, j)
        // Simulate work
        time.Sleep(time.Millisecond * 100)
        results <- j * 2 // Example processing: double the job value
    }
}
```

```go
func fanOutExample() {
    const numJobs = 5
    jobs := make(chan int, numJobs)
    results := make(chan int, numJobs)

    // Launch a fixed number of workers
    for w := 1; w <= 3; w++ {
        go worker(w, jobs, results)
    }

    // Send jobs to the workers
    for j := 1; j <= numJobs; j++ {
        jobs <- j
    }
    close(jobs)

    // Collect results (can be part of the Fan-In pattern)
    for a := 1; a <= numJobs; a++ {
        res := <-results
        fmt.Println("Result:", res)
    }
}
```

In this example, three worker goroutines process jobs concurrently, demonstrating the Fan-Out pattern.

Fan-In Pattern

Purpose:

The Fan-In pattern aggregates data from multiple channels into a single channel. This is useful when multiple concurrent tasks produce results, and you need to combine these results for further processing or output.

How It Works:

Multiple channels or goroutines produce results.

A single aggregator function reads from these channels concurrently and writes the outputs into a single, unified channel.

Consumers can then process results from the unified channel without needing to handle multiple sources.

Example:

go
Copy code

```go
func merge(channels ...<-chan int) <-chan int {
    var wg sync.WaitGroup
    merged := make(chan int)

    output := func(ch <-chan int) {
        for v := range ch {
            merged <- v
        }
        wg.Done()
    }

    wg.Add(len(channels))
    for _, ch := range channels {
        go output(ch)
    }

    // Close the merged channel once all channels are drained.
    go func() {
        wg.Wait()
        close(merged)
    }()

    return merged
}
```

```go
func fanInExample() {
    ch1 := make(chan int)
    ch2 := make(chan int)

    // Simulate two producers
    go func() {
        for i := 1; i <= 3; i++ {
            ch1 <- i
            time.Sleep(time.Millisecond * 50)
        }
        close(ch1)
    }()

    go func() {
        for i := 4; i <= 6; i++ {
            ch2 <- i
            time.Sleep(time.Millisecond * 70)
        }
        close(ch2)
    }()

    // Merge results from both channels
    for v := range merge(ch1, ch2) {
        fmt.Println("Merged value:", v)
    }
```

```
}
```

In this example, two channels are merged into one using the merge function. The merged channel produces a unified stream of values from both channels, illustrating the Fan-In pattern.

Benefits and Use Cases

Improved Throughput:

By distributing tasks across multiple workers (Fan-Out) and then aggregating the results (Fan-In), you can achieve higher parallelism and better resource utilization.

Simplified Coordination:

These patterns reduce the complexity of managing multiple concurrent goroutines, making your code more modular and easier to maintain.

Scalability:

Both patterns are adaptable: you can adjust the number of workers in Fan-Out or the number of producing channels in

Fan-In based on your application's load and system capabilities.

Conclusion

Fan-Out and Fan-In are powerful concurrency patterns in Go that facilitate the distribution of work and the aggregation of results, respectively. By using these patterns, you can design systems that efficiently process high volumes of tasks in parallel, ultimately leading to improved performance, responsiveness, and scalability in concurrent applications.

8.3 Context Package for Cancellation and Timeouts

The context package in Go is a powerful tool for managing cancellation, deadlines, and request-scoped values across API boundaries and between goroutines. It provides a standard way to signal that work should be abandoned—whether due to a timeout, explicit cancellation, or other contextual reasons—which is especially useful in distributed systems and concurrent applications.

Key Features of the Context Package

Cancellation Propagation:

Contexts allow you to propagate cancellation signals across multiple goroutines. When a context is canceled, all goroutines using that context can detect the cancellation and stop their work promptly. This is achieved using the Done() channel that every context provides.

Timeouts and Deadlines:

You can create contexts that automatically cancel after a specific duration (WithTimeout) or at a specific time (WithDeadline). This is particularly useful to prevent operations from hanging indefinitely. When the timeout or deadline is reached, the context is canceled, and subsequent calls to Err() will return a timeout or deadline exceeded error.

Request-Scoped Data:

Although not the primary focus in cancellation and timeouts, the context package also allows you to store request-scoped values. This makes it useful for passing configuration or metadata (like authentication tokens) across function calls.

Creating Contexts for Cancellation and Timeouts

Using context.WithCancel:

This function creates a derived context that can be canceled manually. It returns a cancel function that, when called, cancels the context and notifies all goroutines waiting on its Done() channel.

```go
Copy code
ctx, cancel := context.WithCancel(context.Background())
defer cancel() // Ensure resources are cleaned up when done

go func() {
    // Simulate some work
    time.Sleep(2 * time.Second)
    cancel() // Cancel the context after some condition
}()
```

```go
<-ctx.Done() // Wait for the cancellation signal
fmt.Println("Context canceled:", ctx.Err())
```

Using context.WithTimeout:

This function creates a context that will be automatically canceled after a given duration. It's useful for setting a maximum time limit on operations.

go
Copy code

```go
ctx, cancel := context.WithTimeout(context.Background(),
3*time.Second)
defer cancel()

select {
case <-time.After(5 * time.Second):
   fmt.Println("Operation completed")
case <-ctx.Done():
   fmt.Println("Operation timed out:", ctx.Err())
}
```

Using context.WithDeadline:

Similar to WithTimeout, this function creates a context that is canceled at a specific point in time rather than after a duration.

```go
go
Copy code
deadline := time.Now().Add(3 * time.Second)
ctx, cancel := context.WithDeadline(context.Background(), deadline)
defer cancel()

// Use the context in subsequent operations...
select {
case <-time.After(5 * time.Second):
    fmt.Println("Operation completed")
case <-ctx.Done():
    fmt.Println("Operation exceeded deadline:", ctx.Err())
}
```

Best Practices

Pass Contexts as the First Parameter:

In Go, it is idiomatic to pass contexts as the first argument to functions that require cancellation or timeout control. For example:

```go
Copy code
func fetchData(ctx context.Context, url string) (Data, error) {
    // Use ctx for cancellation and deadlines in HTTP requests or database calls.
}
```

Don't Store Contexts in Structs:

Contexts should be passed explicitly through function parameters rather than stored in global variables or struct fields. This ensures that each operation is aware of its own cancellation and timeout policies.

Handle Context Cancellation Appropriately:

Always check for context cancellation (via ctx.Done()) within long-running operations. Respond to cancellation by cleaning up resources and exiting the function as soon as possible.

Defer Cancelation:

When creating a context with WithCancel, WithTimeout, or WithDeadline, ensure you defer the cancel function. This prevents resource leaks, even if the operation completes before the context is canceled.

Conclusion

The context package in Go provides a standardized way to manage cancellation and timeouts across concurrent operations. By using contexts, you can ensure that your applications handle long-running tasks, timeouts, and cancellations gracefully, improving reliability and responsiveness. Understanding and applying these patterns is essential for building robust, concurrent systems that behave well under load and in distributed environments.

8.4 Avoiding Common Concurrency Pitfalls

Concurrency in Go can lead to powerful, high-performance applications, but it also introduces potential pitfalls that can compromise the correctness and efficiency of your programs. Being aware of these common issues—and employing strategies to avoid them—is crucial. Here are some key pitfalls and tips for avoiding them:

1. Data Races

The Pitfall:

When multiple goroutines access shared data without proper synchronization, unexpected behavior and hard-to-reproduce bugs (data races) may occur.

How to Avoid:

Use Channels:

Communicate between goroutines by passing data through channels instead of sharing memory.
Synchronization Primitives:
Use mutexes (e.g., sync.Mutex, sync.RWMutex) to protect shared data.

Race Detector:

Run your code with Go's race detector (go run -race or go test -race) during development to catch data races early.

2. Deadlocks

The Pitfall:

Deadlocks occur when two or more goroutines are waiting on each other to release resources, causing the program to stall indefinitely.

How to Avoid:

Careful Locking:

Ensure that locks are acquired in a consistent order and held for the minimal duration necessary.

Channel Communication:

When using channels, design your system so that there's always a receiver for every sender. Avoid scenarios where goroutines block indefinitely waiting for input.

Timeouts and Contexts:

Use context.WithTimeout or other cancellation mechanisms to break out of deadlocked situations.

3. Goroutine Leaks

The Pitfall:

Goroutines that are no longer needed but are still waiting (e.g., on a channel read or a blocked operation) can accumulate over time, leading to increased memory usage and eventual performance degradation.

How to Avoid:

Proper Cancellation:

Use contexts or cancellation channels to signal goroutines to exit when their work is done or no longer needed.

Ensure Exit Paths:

When designing goroutines that wait on channels, always include a way to break out of the loop (for example, by detecting a closed channel).

Monitor Goroutine Counts:

Use runtime profiling tools to monitor the number of active goroutines and ensure that they are not growing unexpectedly.

4. Excessive Concurrency

The Pitfall:

Creating an excessive number of goroutines can overwhelm system resources, leading to high memory usage and contention, even if each goroutine is lightweight.

How to Avoid:

Worker Pools:

Limit concurrency by implementing worker pools. Instead of spawning a new goroutine for every task, use a fixed number of workers to process tasks from a shared queue.

Rate Limiting:

Employ techniques like semaphores (using buffered channels) to control the rate at which goroutines are launched.

5. Misuse of Channels

The Pitfall:

Incorrect channel operations—such as closing a channel multiple times, not closing a channel when necessary, or mismanaging buffered channels—can lead to unexpected behavior or runtime panics.

How to Avoid:

Single Closure:

Ensure that only the sender (or a designated coordinator) is responsible for closing a channel.

Design Clarity:

Clearly document whether a channel is used for one-way communication (send-only or receive-only) to prevent misuse.

Default Cases:

Use default cases in select statements carefully to avoid unintended non-blocking behavior.

Conclusion

Avoiding common concurrency pitfalls in Go requires a mix of careful design, proper use of synchronization primitives, and diligent testing. By using channels for safe communication, employing mutexes and other synchronization tools to prevent data races and deadlocks, and by managing goroutine lifecycles through contexts and worker pools, you can build concurrent applications that are both efficient and robust. Regular use of profiling and race detection tools further ensures that issues are caught early, allowing you to maintain a healthy, scalable codebase.

Chapter 9
Building Scalable Applications

Building scalable applications in Go involves designing your system to handle increasing load and complexity while maintaining performance and reliability. Key strategies include:

Design for Concurrency:

Leverage Go's lightweight goroutines and channels to enable parallel processing. This built-in concurrency model helps you efficiently utilize multi-core systems.

Horizontal Scaling and Load Balancing:

Architect your application so that it can run across multiple servers. Employ load balancing techniques to distribute traffic evenly, ensuring no single instance becomes a bottleneck.

Microservices Architecture:

Decompose your application into smaller, independent services. This modularity allows each component to scale independently, simplifies maintenance, and enhances fault isolation.

Caching and Distributed Systems:

Implement caching strategies to reduce database load and improve response times. Use distributed systems and message queues to manage state and coordinate across services.

By combining these approaches with continuous profiling, monitoring, and iterative optimization, you can build Go applications that scale effectively and respond gracefully to growing demands.

9.1 Designing for Scalability

Designing for scalability involves creating a software architecture that can gracefully handle increased load, data volume, and user demand without significant degradation in performance. Here are some key strategies for designing scalable applications in Go:

Modular and Decoupled Architecture:

Build your application as a collection of independent, loosely coupled components or microservices. This modular design allows each service to scale independently, simplifies maintenance, and enhances fault tolerance by isolating failures.

Statelessness:

Favor stateless services where possible. Stateless components are easier to replicate horizontally since they do not depend on local session data, allowing load balancers to distribute traffic evenly across instances.

Efficient Concurrency:

Leverage Go's native concurrency model using goroutines and channels. Efficiently designed concurrent code can handle multiple requests simultaneously, maximizing the use of available CPU cores and improving overall throughput.

Load Balancing and Horizontal Scaling:

Design your system to run across multiple servers. Use load balancing techniques to distribute incoming requests and monitor service performance to add or remove instances dynamically based on demand.

Caching and Asynchronous Processing:

Implement caching strategies to reduce the load on back-end systems and improve response times. Use asynchronous processing (e.g., message queues, background workers) to decouple heavy processing tasks from the request path, allowing your system to handle spikes in traffic more gracefully.

Scalable Data Management:

Choose data storage solutions that can scale horizontally, such as distributed databases or NoSQL systems. Design your data access patterns to support sharding, replication, and efficient querying to meet growing data demands.

Monitoring and Profiling:
Incorporate robust monitoring, logging, and profiling tools (like pprof, Prometheus, or Grafana) early in the development process. These tools help you identify performance bottlenecks and optimize critical paths as your system scales.

By focusing on modularity, statelessness, and efficient resource management, you can design Go applications that not only meet current demands but also adapt to future growth with minimal rework.

9.2 Load Balancing and Horizontal Scaling

Load balancing and horizontal scaling are essential strategies for building resilient, high-performance systems that can handle increasing traffic and workload demands.

Load Balancing

Definition:

Load balancing distributes incoming network traffic across multiple servers or instances, ensuring that no single server is overwhelmed. This improves system reliability, responsiveness, and availability.

Techniques:

DNS-Based Load Balancing: Distributes traffic by resolving a domain name to different IP addresses.

Hardware Load Balancers: Dedicated appliances that efficiently route traffic.

Software Load Balancers: Tools like Nginx, HAProxy, or cloud-based load balancing services that distribute requests based on various algorithms (e.g., round-robin, least connections, weighted distribution).

Benefits:

Improved Availability: If one instance fails, others can continue handling the load.

Optimized Resource Utilization: Evenly spreads out traffic, reducing the risk of server overload.

Enhanced Scalability: Allows you to add or remove servers seamlessly based on demand.

Horizontal Scaling

Definition:

Horizontal scaling (or scaling out) involves adding more servers or instances to your system to handle increased load. This contrasts with vertical scaling, which means increasing the resources (CPU, memory) of a single server.

Approach:

Stateless Services: Design your services to be stateless so that any instance can handle any request. This makes it easier to distribute the load.

Microservices Architecture: Decompose your application into smaller, independent services that can be scaled individually.

Containerization and Orchestration: Technologies like Docker and Kubernetes simplify horizontal scaling by managing containerized applications across clusters of servers.

Benefits:

Scalability: Easily add more instances to support growth.

Fault Tolerance: Distributes risk by spreading the load across multiple servers. If one server fails, others can continue to serve requests.
Cost-Effective: Scale out using commodity hardware or cloud instances, which can be more economical than high-end, vertically scaled machines.

Combined Strategy

By combining load balancing with horizontal scaling, you create a system that:

Dynamically Adapts: Can automatically adjust the number of active servers in response to real-time load, often using auto-scaling groups in cloud environments.

Ensures Resilience: Maintains high availability and fault tolerance, as the failure of a single instance is mitigated by the presence of multiple healthy instances.

Maximizes Performance: Efficiently distributes requests, ensuring that each server is optimally utilized without becoming a performance bottleneck.

Conclusion

Load balancing and horizontal scaling are crucial for building scalable applications. They allow you to distribute traffic efficiently, add capacity seamlessly, and create a resilient system that can grow alongside your user base. Whether you're using traditional load balancers or modern orchestration tools like Kubernetes, these strategies are key to handling increased demand while maintaining performance and reliability.

9.3 Using Go with Microservices Architecture

Using Go for microservices architecture leverages the language's simplicity, performance, and built-in concurrency to build scalable, maintainable, and efficient distributed systems. Here's an overview of how Go fits into a microservices environment:

1. Lightweight and Efficient
Fast Compilation and Execution:

Go compiles quickly and produces efficient binaries that run with minimal overhead. This makes it ideal for services that need to start rapidly and perform under heavy load.

Built-In Concurrency:

Goroutines and channels simplify concurrent programming, enabling microservices to handle multiple requests simultaneously without the complexity of traditional threading models.

2. Simplicity and Maintainability

Clean Syntax:

Go's minimalistic syntax and straightforward design reduce the learning curve and improve code readability. This is especially beneficial in microservices, where multiple teams may contribute to different services.

Standard Library and Tools:

Go's rich standard library and ecosystem (including tools like go fmt, go test, and go mod) streamline development, testing, and dependency management, ensuring that each microservice can be developed and maintained independently.

3. Scalability and Resilience

Statelessness and Isolation:

Microservices built in Go are often designed to be stateless, making them easier to replicate and scale horizontally using load balancing and orchestration tools like Kubernetes.

Robust Communication:

Go's strong support for network programming—via HTTP, gRPC, or other protocols—enables efficient inter-service communication. This is critical for microservices, where services must reliably exchange data.

Fault Tolerance:

Using patterns like circuit breakers, retries, and timeouts (often implemented with Go's context package), microservices can gracefully handle failures, ensuring that issues in one service do not cascade across the system.

4. Ecosystem and Integration

Containerization and Cloud-Native:
Go's static binaries and minimal runtime dependencies make it an excellent choice for containerized environments. Services written in Go are easily packaged with Docker and deployed in cloud-native architectures.

Microservices Frameworks:

Several frameworks and libraries in the Go ecosystem (e.g., Go Kit, Micro, and Gizmo) provide abstractions and utilities specifically designed for microservices, including service discovery, load balancing, and distributed tracing.

Conclusion

Using Go with microservices architecture allows developers to build systems that are fast, scalable, and resilient. The language's efficiency, simplicity, and excellent support for concurrency make it well-suited for developing independent, loosely coupled services. Whether you're building RESTful APIs, gRPC services, or event-driven systems, Go provides a robust foundation for modern, cloud-native microservices applications.

9.4 Caching Strategies and Distributed Systems

Caching strategies play a critical role in distributed systems by improving performance, reducing latency, and lowering the load on primary data stores. In a distributed environment, where data is spread across multiple nodes or services, caching must be designed carefully to balance consistency, availability, and scalability. Here are some key concepts and strategies:

1. Types of Caching

Local (In-Memory) Caching:

Each node or service maintains its own cache, which can provide very fast access times. However, this approach may lead to data inconsistency across nodes unless additional synchronization is implemented.

Distributed Caching:

A shared cache, such as Redis or Memcached, is accessible by multiple nodes. This centralizes cache management, simplifies consistency, and often supports features like replication and high availability.

2. Caching Strategies

Write-Through Caching:

In this strategy, data is written to both the cache and the underlying data store simultaneously. It ensures that the cache remains consistent with the database but can introduce write latency.

Write-Back (Write-Behind) Caching:

Data is written to the cache first, and the database is updated asynchronously. This can improve write performance, but it requires careful management of potential data loss or inconsistency in case of failures.

Write-Around Caching:

Data is written directly to the database, bypassing the cache. This is useful when write operations are infrequent, ensuring that the cache contains only frequently accessed data while avoiding cache pollution.

Cache Invalidation:

Keeping cached data fresh is essential. Techniques include time-to-live (TTL) policies, explicit invalidation (removing outdated entries when data changes), or using event-driven mechanisms to update caches in real time.

3. Cache Eviction Policies

Least Recently Used (LRU):

Removes the least recently accessed items first, assuming that data accessed recently is more likely to be requested again.

Least Frequently Used (LFU):

Removes items that are accessed less frequently, ensuring that commonly used data remains in the cache.

First-In, First-Out (FIFO):

Evicts the oldest items in the cache first, which can be simpler to implement but may not always reflect actual usage patterns.

4. Considerations for Distributed Systems

Consistency Models:

Distributed caches must often balance strong consistency with high availability. Eventual consistency is common, where updates propagate over time, but some systems may require stricter guarantees.

Data Partitioning:

Sharding data across multiple cache nodes can improve scalability and performance. Consistent hashing is a common technique to distribute keys evenly and allow smooth scaling as nodes are added or removed.

Fault Tolerance and Replication:

To ensure high availability, distributed caches often replicate data across multiple nodes. This redundancy allows the system to continue operating even if a node fails.

Latency Considerations:

Caching reduces the need to access slower, centralized data stores. In distributed systems, strategically placing caches closer to the end users (edge caching) can further reduce response times.

Conclusion

Implementing effective caching strategies in distributed systems is essential for achieving high performance and scalability. By choosing the right caching approach—whether local or distributed, and the appropriate eviction and invalidation policies—you can significantly improve response times, reduce backend load, and ensure a more responsive and resilient application architecture.

Part IV: Real-World Applications

Chapter 10
Building Web Applications

Building web applications in Go is streamlined by the language's powerful standard library and its focus on simplicity and performance. Here's a brief overview of key aspects:

HTTP Server:

Go's built-in net/http package makes it easy to create robust HTTP servers. You can quickly set up request handlers and serve static or dynamic content with minimal code.

Routing and Middleware:

Basic routing is handled by http.ServeMux, while third-party routers like Gorilla Mux offer advanced features such as URL parameters and more flexible patterns. Middleware patterns allow you to intercept and modify requests or responses for logging, authentication, or error handling.

RESTful APIs and JSON:

Building RESTful APIs is straightforward. Go's native support for JSON encoding/decoding via the encoding/json package helps in constructing APIs that communicate using JSON.

Template Rendering:

The html/template package enables server-side rendering of HTML pages with dynamic data, making it easier to build web applications with integrated views.

Performance and Concurrency:

Thanks to goroutines and channels, Go can handle multiple web requests concurrently, ensuring high performance and responsiveness even under heavy load.

Testing and Deployment:

The language's testing tools, such as go test, along with its ability to compile into a single binary, simplify both testing and deployment of web applications.

Overall, Go's efficiency, ease of use, and rich ecosystem make it an excellent choice for building scalable and high-performance web applications.

10.1 Creating HTTP Servers with net/http

The Go standard library's net/http package provides a simple, yet powerful framework for building HTTP servers. Here's an overview of how to create HTTP servers with net/http:

1. Basic HTTP Server

At its core, an HTTP server in Go listens for incoming connections and routes them to handler functions that process requests and write responses. The simplest server can be set up with just a few lines of code:

```go
go
Copy code
package main

import (
  "fmt"
  "net/http"
)

func helloHandler(w http.ResponseWriter, r *http.Request) {
  fmt.Fprintln(w, "Hello, World!")
}

func main() {
  http.HandleFunc("/", helloHandler)
  // Start the server on port 8080.
  fmt.Println("Server is listening on port 8080")
  if err := http.ListenAndServe(":8080", nil); err != nil {
    fmt.Println("Error starting server:", err)
  }
}
http.HandleFunc:
```

This function registers a handler function for a given URL pattern. In the example above, all requests to the root path (/) are handled by helloHandler.

http.ListenAndServe:

This function starts the server on the specified port. The second argument is a handler; passing nil uses the default multiplexer.

2. Creating Custom Handlers

For more complex applications, you might define custom types that implement the http.Handler interface, which requires a ServeHTTP(w http.ResponseWriter, r *http.Request) method:

```go
Copy code
type myHandler struct{}

func (h *myHandler) ServeHTTP(w http.ResponseWriter, r *http.Request) {
    fmt.Fprintln(w, "Response from myHandler")
}
```

```go
func main() {
    handler := &myHandler{}
    http.Handle("/custom", handler)
    fmt.Println("Server is listening on port 8080")
    http.ListenAndServe(":8080", nil)
}
```

This approach promotes code organization and reusability when handling multiple routes or complex logic.

3. Routing and Multiplexing

The default http.ServeMux allows you to map URL patterns to different handlers. You can register multiple routes like this:

```go
go
Copy code
func aboutHandler(w http.ResponseWriter, r *http.Request) {
    fmt.Fprintln(w, "About page")
}

func main() {
    mux := http.NewServeMux()
```

```go
mux.HandleFunc("/", helloHandler)
mux.HandleFunc("/about", aboutHandler)

fmt.Println("Server is listening on port 8080")
http.ListenAndServe(":8080", mux)
}
```

Using a custom ServeMux can help you manage routes more cleanly, especially in larger applications.

4. Middleware and Wrapping Handlers

Middleware functions wrap handlers to add common functionality (like logging, authentication, etc.) before passing the request along. For example:

go
Copy code
```go
func loggingMiddleware(next http.Handler) http.Handler {
    return http.HandlerFunc(func(w http.ResponseWriter, r
*http.Request) {
    fmt.Printf("Request: %s %s\n", r.Method, r.URL.Path)
    next.ServeHTTP(w, r)
  })
}
```

```go
func main() {
    mux := http.NewServeMux()
    mux.HandleFunc("/", helloHandler)

    // Wrap the default mux with logging middleware.
    loggedMux := loggingMiddleware(mux)

    fmt.Println("Server is listening on port 8080")
    http.ListenAndServe(":8080", loggedMux)
}
```

This pattern allows you to modularly add cross-cutting concerns without cluttering your core handler logic.

5. Graceful Shutdown and Advanced Features

For production-grade servers, you might want to implement graceful shutdown, TLS support, and request timeouts. The net/http package integrates with context and other packages to facilitate these needs.

For example, to implement graceful shutdown:

go

```
Copy code
package main

import (
    "context"
    "fmt"
    "net/http"
    "os"
    "os/signal"
    "time"
)

func helloHandler(w http.ResponseWriter, r *http.Request)
{
    fmt.Fprintln(w, "Hello, World!")
}

func main() {
    mux := http.NewServeMux()
    mux.HandleFunc("/", helloHandler)

    server := &http.Server{
        Addr:    ":8080",
        Handler: mux,
    }
```

```go
// Run server in a goroutine.
go func() {
    fmt.Println("Server is listening on port 8080")
    if err := server.ListenAndServe(); err != nil && err !=
http.ErrServerClosed {
        fmt.Println("Server error:", err)
    }
}()

// Listen for interrupt signal to gracefully shut down.
stop := make(chan os.Signal, 1)
signal.Notify(stop, os.Interrupt)
<-stop

fmt.Println("Shutting down server...")
ctx, cancel :=
context.WithTimeout(context.Background(),
5*time.Second)
defer cancel()

if err := server.Shutdown(ctx); err != nil {
    fmt.Println("Error during shutdown:", err)
}
fmt.Println("Server gracefully stopped")
```

}

This example uses the http.Server.Shutdown method to allow the server to complete active requests before closing.

Conclusion

Creating HTTP servers with Go's net/http package is both straightforward and flexible. Whether you're building a simple web page or a complex API, Go provides the tools—handlers, routing, middleware, and graceful shutdown—to build robust, high-performance web applications.

10.2 Routing with gorilla/mux and http.ServeMux

Routing in Go can be handled using the built-in http.ServeMux or more advanced third-party routers like Gorilla Mux. Both have their strengths and can be chosen based on the complexity of your application.

http.ServeMux

Built-In Simplicity:

http.ServeMux is part of Go's standard library and offers a straightforward way to map URL patterns to handler functions. It works well for simple applications with static or basic dynamic routes.

Pattern Matching:

It supports basic path matching where patterns are matched by prefix. For example, registering "/" as a handler will match all routes, while more specific paths (like "/about") can override the general pattern.

Example:

```go
Copy code
package main

import (
    "fmt"
```

```go
    "net/http"
)

func homeHandler(w http.ResponseWriter, r *http.Request) {
    fmt.Fprintln(w, "Welcome Home!")
}

func aboutHandler(w http.ResponseWriter, r *http.Request) {
    fmt.Fprintln(w, "About Page")
}

func main() {
    mux := http.NewServeMux()
    mux.HandleFunc("/", homeHandler)
    mux.HandleFunc("/about", aboutHandler)

    fmt.Println("Server is running on :8080")
    http.ListenAndServe(":8080", mux)
}
```
This approach is lightweight and effective for basic routing needs.

Gorilla Mux

Advanced Features:

Gorilla Mux is a powerful third-party router that provides features beyond what http.ServeMux offers. It supports complex pattern matching, route variables, and regular expressions in paths.

Dynamic Routing:

With Gorilla Mux, you can define routes with parameters that are extracted from the URL. This is especially useful for RESTful APIs where resource identifiers are part of the URL.

Example:

```go
Copy code
package main

import (
    "fmt"
    "log"
    "net/http"
```

```go
    "github.com/gorilla/mux"
)

func homeHandler(w http.ResponseWriter, r
*http.Request) {
  fmt.Fprintln(w, "Welcome Home!")
}

func articleHandler(w http.ResponseWriter, r
*http.Request) {
  vars := mux.Vars(r)
  articleID := vars["id"]
  fmt.Fprintf(w, "Article ID: %s\n", articleID)
}

func main() {
  router := mux.NewRouter()
  router.HandleFunc("/", homeHandler)
  // Route with a variable 'id'
  router.HandleFunc("/articles/{id}", articleHandler)

  fmt.Println("Server is running on :8080")
  log.Fatal(http.ListenAndServe(":8080", router))
}
```

In this example, the /articles/{id} route captures the article ID from the URL, which can then be accessed via mux.Vars(r).

Additional Capabilities:

Gorilla Mux also supports middleware, named routes, and custom matchers, making it ideal for larger, more complex applications that require flexible routing logic.

Conclusion

Use http.ServeMux when you need a simple, built-in solution with minimal dependencies for straightforward routing.
Choose Gorilla Mux for more complex applications that require dynamic URL parameters, advanced matching rules, or additional features like middleware.

Both options integrate seamlessly with Go's net/http package, so you can pick the one that best fits your project's requirements.

10.3 Middleware and Request Handling

Middleware in Go provides a way to intercept, modify, or augment HTTP requests and responses as they pass through the server. It allows you to encapsulate common functionality—such as logging, authentication, error handling, and request tracing—in reusable components that wrap your core request handlers.

How Middleware Works

Middleware functions typically take an http.Handler as input and return a new http.Handler. This wrapper pattern enables you to process the request before or after the core handler executes, or even short-circuit the request entirely if certain conditions aren't met.

Basic Middleware Structure:

```go
Copy code
func loggingMiddleware(next http.Handler) http.Handler {
```

```go
    return http.HandlerFunc(func(w http.ResponseWriter, r
*http.Request) {
        log.Printf("Received %s request for %s", r.Method,
r.URL.Path)
    // Call the next handler in the chain
    next.ServeHTTP(w, r)
  })
}
```

In this example, loggingMiddleware logs the incoming request and then calls the next handler in the chain.

Chaining Middleware

Middleware can be chained together so that multiple layers of functionality are applied to each request. For example, you might want to log requests, enforce authentication, and then finally handle the request:

```go
go
Copy code
func authMiddleware(next http.Handler) http.Handler {
    return http.HandlerFunc(func(w http.ResponseWriter, r
*http.Request) {
        if r.Header.Get("Authorization") == "" {
```

```go
                        http.Error(w,    "Unauthorized",
http.StatusUnauthorized)
        return
    }
    next.ServeHTTP(w, r)
  })
}

func finalHandler(w http.ResponseWriter, r *http.Request)
{
    fmt.Fprintln(w, "Hello, authenticated user!")
}

func main() {
    // Create the final handler
    final := http.HandlerFunc(finalHandler)

    // Wrap the final handler with authentication and logging
middleware
    handler := loggingMiddleware(authMiddleware(final))

    http.Handle("/", handler)
    log.Println("Server is running on :8080")
    http.ListenAndServe(":8080", nil)
}
```

Here, each request passes first through the logging middleware, then through the authentication middleware, before reaching the final handler.

Middleware in Third-Party Routers

Frameworks like Gorilla Mux make it even easier to integrate middleware. They often provide helper functions to apply middleware globally or on a per-route basis:

```go
go
Copy code
router := mux.NewRouter()
router.HandleFunc("/dashboard",
dashboardHandler).Methods("GET")

// Apply middleware globally
router.Use(loggingMiddleware)
router.Use(authMiddleware)

http.ListenAndServe(":8080", router)
```

This approach centralizes common functionality without having to manually wrap each handler.

Request Handling Essentials

In Go, a request handler is any function that satisfies the signature:

```go
Copy code
func(w http.ResponseWriter, r *http.Request)
```

or implements the http.Handler interface. Within a handler, you can:

Read Request Data:

Access query parameters (r.URL.Query()), headers (r.Header), or the request body.

Write Responses:

Use w.Write() or helper functions like fmt.Fprintln() to send data back to the client. You can also set headers with w.Header().Set("Content-Type", "application/json").

Handle Errors:

Use http.Error() to send standardized error responses.

Benefits of Using Middleware

Reusability:

Write once and apply across multiple endpoints, reducing code duplication.

Separation of Concerns:

Isolate cross-cutting concerns like logging, authentication, and error handling from the core business logic.

Flexibility:

Easily add, remove, or modify middleware layers as your application requirements evolve.

Conclusion

Middleware in Go is a powerful pattern that enhances the modularity and maintainability of web applications. By wrapping request handlers with reusable middleware components, you can manage common tasks such as logging, authentication, and error handling in a clean, centralized way—ultimately leading to more organized and scalable server code.

10.4 Building RESTful APIs

Building RESTful APIs in Go leverages the language's simplicity, performance, and rich standard library to create scalable and maintainable services. Here are some key considerations and best practices:

1. Designing API Endpoints

Resource-Oriented URLs:
Structure your URLs to represent resources clearly, e.g., /users, /orders/{id}, or /products/{id}/reviews. Use plural nouns and standard HTTP verbs (GET, POST, PUT, DELETE) to indicate operations on these resources.

Versioning:

Consider including a version in your URL (e.g., /api/v1/users) to ensure backward compatibility when the API evolves.

2. Request Handling and Routing

Using net/http:

The built-in net/http package allows you to set up handlers for various endpoints. For simple APIs, you can use http.HandleFunc and http.ServeMux to map URL patterns to functions.

Advanced Routing with Gorilla Mux or Chi

:For more complex routing needs, third-party routers like Gorilla Mux or Chi provide flexible pattern matching, route variables, and middleware support. For example, Gorilla Mux enables you to extract URL parameters easily:

```go
Copy code
router := mux.NewRouter()
router.HandleFunc("/users/{id}",
userHandler).Methods("GET")
```

3. JSON Encoding and Decoding

Marshalling and Unmarshalling:
Go's encoding/json package simplifies converting between Go structs and JSON. Annotate your structs with JSON tags to control key names and omit empty values:

```go
Copy code
type User struct {
    ID    int    `json:"id"`
    Name  string `json:"name"`
    Email string `json:"email,omitempty"`
}
```

Use json.NewDecoder(r.Body).Decode(&user) to parse request bodies and json.NewEncoder(w).Encode(response) to send JSON responses.

4. Error Handling and Status Codes

Consistent Responses:

Return appropriate HTTP status codes (e.g., 200 OK, 201 Created, 400 Bad Request, 404 Not Found, 500 Internal Server Error) to indicate success or failure.

Error Messages:

Standardize error responses in JSON format. For example:

```json
Copy code
{ "error": "User not found", "code": 404 }
```
This helps clients interpret the response easily.

5. Middleware and Cross-Cutting Concerns

Reusable Middleware:

Implement middleware for logging, authentication, rate limiting, and CORS. Middleware wraps handlers to inject common functionality without cluttering core business logic.

```go
Copy code
func loggingMiddleware(next http.Handler) http.Handler {
```

```
return http.HandlerFunc(func(w http.ResponseWriter, r
*http.Request) {
    log.Printf("%s %s", r.Method, r.RequestURI)
    next.ServeHTTP(w, r)
  })
}
```

Chaining Handlers:

Most routers allow you to apply middleware globally or per route, simplifying the integration of these cross-cutting concerns.

6. Testing and Documentation

Automated Testing:

Use Go's testing framework (go test) to write unit tests for your handlers and integration tests for API endpoints. Tools like Postman or cURL can also help verify API behavior.

API Documentation:

Generate or write documentation for your API endpoints using tools like Swagger/OpenAPI. This facilitates client integration and helps maintain consistency as your API evolves.

Conclusion

Building RESTful APIs in Go is straightforward due to the language's efficient standard libraries, powerful routing capabilities, and excellent support for concurrency. By following REST conventions, handling JSON effectively, implementing robust error handling, and utilizing middleware for common concerns, you can create scalable, maintainable APIs that serve as the backbone of modern web and mobile applications.

Chapter 11
Working with Databases

Working with databases in Go involves leveraging the language's robust ecosystem and built-in packages to interact with both SQL and NoSQL systems. Go's standard library provides the database/sql package, which offers a generic interface for SQL databases and supports connection pooling, transactions, and prepared statements. This package is complemented by drivers for various databases like MySQL, PostgreSQL, and SQLite, making it straightforward to connect and execute queries.

For more advanced data handling, many developers turn to ORMs (Object-Relational Mappers) such as GORM or use query builders like sqlx. These libraries abstract some of the boilerplate code involved in writing SQL queries, allowing you to work with database records as Go structs while still enabling fine-grained control when needed.

Beyond SQL, Go also supports NoSQL databases like MongoDB through drivers that provide idiomatic interfaces. When working with NoSQL, it's important to understand the specific data models and query languages of these databases to design efficient and scalable data access patterns.

Best practices for working with databases in Go include proper error handling, managing database connections responsibly, and using transactions when multiple operations must succeed or fail together. Additionally, integrating database migrations into your workflow—using tools like Goose or Flyway—helps maintain schema consistency across different environments.

Overall, Go's powerful standard library, combined with its vibrant ecosystem of third-party libraries, enables developers to build efficient and scalable applications that interact seamlessly with various database systems.

11.1 Connecting to SQL and NoSQL Databases

Connecting to SQL and NoSQL databases in Go involves different approaches and libraries, each tailored to the type of database you are working with. Below is an overview of how to connect to SQL databases using the database/sql package and to NoSQL databases using dedicated drivers or client libraries.

Connecting to SQL Databases

Go's standard library includes the database/sql package, which provides a generic interface for interacting with SQL databases. To connect to a specific SQL database, you'll also need the corresponding driver.

Steps to Connect:

Import the SQL Package and Driver:
For example, if you're connecting to MySQL, you might import:

```go
Copy code
import (
    "database/sql"
    _ "github.com/go-sql-driver/mysql" // MySQL driver
```

)

Open a Connection:

Use sql.Open to establish a connection. Note that sql.Open does not immediately create a connection to the database—it prepares a pool of connections for you.

```go
Copy code
db, err := sql.Open("mysql",
"user:password@tcp(localhost:3306)/dbname")
if err != nil {
   log.Fatal(err)
}
defer db.Close()
```

Ping the Database:

Verify that the connection is live by calling db.Ping().

```go
Copy code
if err := db.Ping(); err != nil {
   log.Fatal("Unable to reach the database:", err)
```

```
}
```

Perform Queries:

Once connected, you can use methods like Query, QueryRow, and Exec to interact with the database.

```go
Copy code
rows, err := db.Query("SELECT id, name FROM users")
if err != nil {
    log.Fatal(err)
}
defer rows.Close()
```

Key Considerations:

Connection Pooling:

The database/sql package manages connection pooling automatically. You can adjust settings with methods like SetMaxOpenConns and SetMaxIdleConns to fine-tune performance.

Prepared Statements:

For improved security and performance, use prepared statements to prevent SQL injection and reuse execution plans.

Connecting to NoSQL Databases

For NoSQL databases, Go developers typically use specialized drivers or client libraries that provide idiomatic interfaces for the target system.

Example: Connecting to MongoDB
MongoDB, a popular document-oriented NoSQL database, offers an official Go driver.

Import the MongoDB Driver:

```go
Copy code
import (
    "context"
    "log"
    "time"
    "go.mongodb.org/mongo-driver/mongo"
```

```
"go.mongodb.org/mongo-driver/mongo/options"
)
```

Establish a Connection:

Use mongo.Connect to connect to your MongoDB instance.

```go
Copy code
ctx, cancel := context.WithTimeout(context.Background(),
10*time.Second)
defer cancel()

client, err := mongo.Connect(ctx,
options.Client().ApplyURI("mongodb://localhost:27017")
)
if err != nil {
    log.Fatal(err)
}
defer client.Disconnect(ctx)
```

Access a Database and Collection:

Once connected, you can interact with the database and collections.

```go
Copy code
collection                                                    :=
client.Database("mydatabase").Collection("users")
// Now you can perform CRUD operations on the
collection.
```

Other NoSQL Databases:

Redis:
Use libraries like go-redis to connect and interact with Redis.
Cassandra, DynamoDB, etc.:
Use community-supported drivers or official SDKs, each with their connection and query patterns.

Conclusion

SQL Databases:

Utilize the database/sql package along with the appropriate driver. This approach provides a robust, standardized way to perform SQL operations with support for connection pooling, transactions, and prepared statements.

NoSQL Databases:
Leverage specialized client libraries (such as MongoDB's official driver) to connect and interact with NoSQL systems, benefiting from interfaces that are designed for the specific data model and query patterns of those databases.

By understanding the tools and patterns for each type of database, you can build applications in Go that efficiently interact with both SQL and NoSQL systems while taking advantage of Go's performance and simplicity.

11.2 Using ORMs and Query Builders

Using ORMs and query builders in Go offers different approaches to interacting with databases. Both strategies aim to simplify database operations but do so in distinct ways, and choosing between them depends on your application's needs and complexity.

Object-Relational Mappers (ORMs)

Overview:
ORMs abstract the underlying SQL queries and enable developers to work with database records as Go structs. This object-relational mapping simplifies CRUD operations, relationship management, and often includes features like migrations, validations, and caching.

Popular ORMs in Go:

GORM:

One of the most widely used ORMs, GORM provides a rich API for working with databases, supporting associations, hooks, transactions, and more.
ent:
A relatively newer ORM that uses code generation to provide type-safe database interactions, making it easy to work with complex data models.

Pop:

Part of the Buffalo framework, Pop is a lightweight ORM focused on simplicity and ease of use.

Pros:

Rapid Development:

ORMs reduce boilerplate code, allowing you to focus on business logic rather than constructing SQL queries.

Abstraction:
They abstract differences between various SQL dialects, making your code more portable.
Relationship Management:
Built-in support for associations (has-one, has-many, many-to-many) simplifies complex data interactions.

Cons:

Performance Overhead:

The abstraction layer can sometimes introduce performance penalties compared to writing raw SQL.
Complexity for Advanced Queries:
For highly optimized or complex queries, ORMs may hide the underlying SQL, making fine-tuning more challenging.

Example Using GORM:

```go
go
Copy code
import (
  "gorm.io/driver/mysql"
  "gorm.io/gorm"
)

type User struct {
  ID   uint `gorm:"primaryKey"`
  Name string
  Email string `gorm:"uniqueIndex"`
}

func main() {
  dsn := "user:password@tcp(127.0.0.1:3306)/dbname?charset=utf8mb4&parseTime=True&loc=Local"
  db, err := gorm.Open(mysql.Open(dsn), &gorm.Config{})
  if err != nil {
    panic("failed to connect database")
  }

  // Automatically migrate schema
```

```go
db.AutoMigrate(&User{})

// Create a new user
user := User{Name: "Alice", Email: "alice@example.com"}
db.Create(&user)

// Query user by email
var result User
db.First(&result, "email = ?", "alice@example.com")
fmt.Println("User found:", result.Name)
}
```

Query Builders

Overview:

Query builders offer a middle ground between raw SQL and full-fledged ORMs. They allow you to programmatically construct SQL queries with a fluent, chainable API while still writing SQL. This approach can result in more readable, maintainable, and type-safe query construction.

Popular Query Builders in Go:

Squirrel:

Provides a fluent API to build SQL queries incrementally. It's lightweight and works with any database driver.

sqlx:

An extension of Go's standard database/sql package, sqlx offers additional features such as struct scanning and named queries, which can simplify working with SQL queries.

Pros:

Fine-Grained Control:

You retain control over the exact SQL generated, which can lead to more optimized queries

Flexibility:Query builders are ideal for constructing complex queries dynamically while minimizing the risk of SQL injection.

Less Overhead:

They introduce less abstraction than ORMs, which can be beneficial for performance-critical applications.

Cons:

More Boilerplate:

Compared to ORMs, query builders require you to manage more aspects of query construction and mapping results to structs.

Less Abstraction for Relationships:

While ORMs manage associations automatically, query builders typically require you to write joins and relationship queries manually.

Example Using Squirrel:

```go
Copy code
import (
    "database/sql"
    "fmt"
    "log"

    sq "github.com/Masterminds/squirrel"
    _ "github.com/go-sql-driver/mysql"
)

type User struct {
    ID   int
```

```go
	Name  string
	Email string
}

func main() {
	db, err := sql.Open("mysql",
"user:password@tcp(localhost:3306)/dbname")
	if err != nil {
		log.Fatal(err)
	}
	defer db.Close()

	// Build a query using Squirrel
	query, args, err := sq.Select("id", "name", "email").
		From("users").
		Where(sq.Eq{"email": "alice@example.com"}).
		ToSql()
	if err != nil {
		log.Fatal(err)
	}

	// Execute the query
	var user User
	err = db.QueryRow(query, args...).Scan(&user.ID,
&user.Name, &user.Email)
```

```go
    if err != nil {
        log.Fatal(err)
    }
    fmt.Println("User found:", user.Name)
}
```

Conclusion

Both ORMs and query builders have their place in Go development:

ORMs are great for rapid development, providing an abstraction layer that simplifies CRUD operations and relationship management.
Query Builders give you more control over your SQL, making them ideal for complex or performance-sensitive queries.
Choosing between the two depends on your specific use case, team expertise, and performance requirements. Many projects even combine both approaches—using an ORM for standard operations and a query builder for custom queries—to strike the right balance between abstraction and control.

11.3 Database Migrations and Connection Pooling

Database migrations and connection pooling are two critical aspects of managing a robust database infrastructure in Go applications.

Database Migrations

Purpose:

Database migrations are version-controlled scripts that modify the schema and sometimes seed data, ensuring that the database evolves in step with application code changes. They help maintain consistency across development, testing, and production environments.

Key Points:

Versioning:

Migrations allow you to track schema changes over time. Each migration is assigned a version number or timestamp, so you can apply, roll back, or reapply changes in a controlled manner.

Tools:

Several popular tools assist with database migrations in Go:

golang-migrate/migrate: A widely used migration library that supports various databases and provides command-line tools.
goose: A migration tool with a simple interface that supports both SQL and Go-based migration scripts.
sql-migrate: Another tool that offers flexibility in managing SQL migrations.

Best Practices:

Keep Migrations Incremental: Write small, incremental migrations rather than large, monolithic ones.
Test Migrations: Ensure that your migration scripts run successfully in development and staging environments before applying them to production.

Automate Deployment: Integrate migration execution into your deployment process to prevent schema mismatches.

Connection Pooling

Purpose:

Connection pooling is the practice of reusing a set of established database connections to serve multiple requests, which improves performance by reducing the overhead of creating and closing connections repeatedly.

How It Works in Go:

Automatic Pooling in database/sql:
Go's database/sql package automatically manages a pool of connections. When you open a database using sql.Open, it doesn't immediately establish a connection; it prepares a pool that lazily creates connections as needed.

Configuring the Pool:
You can fine-tune the connection pool using several methods:

SetMaxOpenConns(n int):

Limits the maximum number of open connections to the database. This is useful to prevent overloading the database server.

SetMaxIdleConns(n int):

Controls the number of idle connections retained in the pool. Keeping idle connections can speed up subsequent queries.

SetConnMaxLifetime(d time.Duration):

Sets the maximum amount of time a connection can remain open. This helps in recycling connections that might become stale or corrupted.

Example:

```go
go
Copy code
db, err := sql.Open("mysql", "user:password@tcp(localhost:3306)/dbname")
if err != nil {
    log.Fatal(err)
```

```
}
// Set pool parameters
db.SetMaxOpenConns(25)
db.SetMaxIdleConns(25)
db.SetConnMaxLifetime(5 * time.Minute)
```

Benefits:

Performance Improvement:

Reduces the latency associated with establishing new connections.

Resource Management:

Helps control resource usage on both the application and database server sides.

Scalability:

Efficient pooling is crucial when dealing with high concurrency, ensuring that connections are reused optimally without overwhelming the database.

Conclusion

By employing database migrations, you ensure that your application's database schema evolves safely and predictably over time. At the same time, proper connection pooling configuration through Go's database/sql package allows your application to efficiently manage database connections, reduce latency, and handle high loads. Together, these practices contribute to a more resilient, performant, and scalable database layer in your Go applications.

11.4 Handling Transactions and Errors

Handling transactions and errors is crucial for building robust, data-consistent applications in Go—especially when interacting with databases. Transactions allow you to execute a series of operations atomically, ensuring that either all operations succeed or none do, thereby preserving data integrity. At the same time, explicit error handling in Go helps you manage unexpected conditions and rollback transactions when necessary.

1. Understanding Transactions

Atomicity:

A transaction groups multiple database operations into a single unit of work. If any operation fails, the entire transaction can be rolled back so that no partial changes persist.

Starting a Transaction:

With Go's database/sql package, you start a transaction by calling db.Begin(), which returns a transaction object (*sql.Tx).

Committing or Rolling Back:

After executing your operations, you call tx.Commit() to save changes or tx.Rollback() to undo them in case of errors.

2. Handling Errors within Transactions

Error handling in Go is explicit. When working with transactions, you must carefully check errors after every operation and decide whether to continue or abort the transaction.

Immediate Error Checks:

After beginning a transaction or executing a query, immediately verify if an error occurred.

Defer Rollback for Safety:

A common idiom is to defer a rollback immediately after starting a transaction. This way, if an error occurs before you commit, the deferred rollback will ensure the transaction is cancelled.

Commit Only on Success:

Only call tx.Commit() if all operations succeed. Otherwise, the deferred rollback (or an explicit call) will clean up any partial changes.

Example:

```go
Copy code
tx, err := db.Begin()
if err != nil {
```

```go
        return fmt.Errorf("failed to begin transaction: %w", err)
    }
    defer func() {
        // Rollback will be a no-op if the transaction is already
committed.
        if err != nil {
            tx.Rollback()
        }
    }()

    // Execute the first query.
    if _, err = tx.Exec("INSERT INTO users(name, email)
VALUES (?, ?)", "Alice", "alice@example.com"); err != nil {
        return fmt.Errorf("failed to insert user: %w", err)
    }

    // Execute a second query that depends on the first.
    if _, err = tx.Exec("INSERT INTO profiles(user_email, bio)
VALUES (?, ?)", "alice@example.com", "Hello, I'm Alice!");
err != nil {
        return fmt.Errorf("failed to insert profile: %w", err)
    }

    // Commit the transaction if all queries succeed.
    if err = tx.Commit(); err != nil {
```

```
    return fmt.Errorf("failed to commit transaction: %w", err)
}
```

```
return nil
```

In this example:

A transaction is started with db.Begin().
Each database operation is executed within the context of the transaction.
Errors are checked immediately. If any error occurs, the deferred function rolls back the transaction.
Only if all operations succeed is tx.Commit() called.

3. Best Practices

Minimize Transaction Scope:
Keep transactions as short as possible to reduce the likelihood of lock contention and to improve performance.

Granular Error Handling:

Check for errors after every operation and wrap them with contextual information. This helps in debugging and understanding exactly where the failure occurred.

Use Context for Timeouts:

Incorporate context (context.Context) in your transaction operations to enforce deadlines and cancellation, ensuring that long-running transactions don't hang indefinitely.

Avoid Nested Transactions:

While some databases support nested transactions (or savepoints), it's generally better to keep transactions flat to avoid complexity.

Conclusion

By combining Go's explicit error handling with careful transaction management, you can build applications that maintain data integrity even in the face of errors. Always ensure that every operation within a transaction is checked for errors and that you have mechanisms in place to roll back changes when something goes wrong. This approach not only safeguards your data but also makes your code more predictable and easier to maintain.

Chapter 12
Cloud-Native Go

Cloud-native Go refers to designing and building Go applications specifically for modern cloud environments. These applications are optimized for scalability, resilience, and efficient resource usage. Key aspects include:

Containerization:

Go's ability to compile into a single static binary makes it an excellent fit for containerization with Docker, ensuring fast startup times and minimal dependencies.

Orchestration:

Cloud-native Go services are often deployed using orchestration platforms like Kubernetes, which manage scaling, load balancing, and service discovery automatically.

Microservices Architecture:

Go's simplicity and strong support for concurrency make it ideal for building microservices, where applications are split into small, independently deployable services that communicate over well-defined APIs.

Observability:

Cloud-native applications incorporate robust monitoring, logging, and tracing (using tools like Prometheus, Grafana, and Jaeger) to ensure performance and facilitate debugging in distributed environments.

Serverless Options:

Go is also used in serverless computing, with cloud providers like AWS Lambda and Google Cloud Functions supporting Go, enabling scalable, event-driven architectures.

By embracing these cloud-native principles, Go applications can achieve high performance and scalability while seamlessly integrating with modern cloud infrastructure.

12.1 Deploying Go Applications to the Cloud

Deploying Go applications to the cloud leverages Go's strengths—its efficiency, fast compile times, and ability to produce a single static binary—to build scalable, maintainable, and high-performance services. Here's an overview of key strategies and best practices for deploying Go applications in cloud environments:

1. Building and Packaging

Static Binaries:

Go applications compile to static binaries that encapsulate all dependencies. This simplifies deployment since you don't need to worry about runtime environments or additional libraries on the target system.

Containerization:

Package your Go application into a Docker container. A typical Dockerfile for a Go application might look like:

Dockerfile
Copy code
```
# Build stage
FROM golang:1.19 as builder
WORKDIR /app
COPY . .
RUN go build -o myapp .

# Run stage
FROM alpine:latest
WORKDIR /app
COPY --from=builder /app/myapp .
ENTRYPOINT ["./myapp"]
```

This multi-stage build minimizes the final image size and ensures a consistent runtime environment.

2. Cloud Deployment Options

Managed Kubernetes:

Use services like Google Kubernetes Engine (GKE), Amazon EKS, or Azure Kubernetes Service (AKS) to orchestrate your containers. Kubernetes automates scaling, load balancing, and rolling updates.

Platform-as-a-Service (PaaS):

Platforms like Google App Engine, AWS Elastic Beanstalk, or Heroku provide simplified deployment processes, handling much of the underlying infrastructure management for you.

Serverless Deployments:

Go is also supported in serverless environments such as AWS Lambda, Google Cloud Functions, or Azure Functions. This model abstracts server management, allowing you to focus solely on code and event-driven architecture.

3. CI/CD Integration

Automation:

Implement continuous integration and deployment pipelines using tools like GitHub Actions, GitLab CI/CD, or Jenkins. Automating tests, builds, and deployments ensures rapid, reliable delivery of updates to production.

Container Registries:

Push your Docker images to cloud-native registries such as Docker Hub, AWS ECR, or Google Container Registry, making them easily accessible for deployment in your orchestration platform.

4. Monitoring, Logging, and Observability

Instrumentation:

Integrate monitoring tools like Prometheus and Grafana to track application metrics, and use distributed tracing solutions such as Jaeger or Zipkin for debugging in microservices environments.

Logging:

Centralize logs using cloud-based logging solutions (e.g., AWS CloudWatch, Google Cloud Logging) or open-source tools like the ELK stack, ensuring that you can efficiently diagnose issues in production.

5. Scalability and Resilience

Auto-Scaling:

Configure your deployment platform to automatically scale based on demand. Kubernetes, for instance, supports horizontal pod autoscaling based on CPU utilization or custom metrics.

Load Balancing:

Use cloud-native load balancers to distribute traffic across instances, ensuring high availability and resilience in the face of increased load or instance failures.

Configuration Management:
Utilize environment variables, configuration files, or secrets management tools (like Kubernetes Secrets or HashiCorp

Vault) to manage environment-specific settings securely and efficiently.

Conclusion

Deploying Go applications to the cloud combines the language's inherent efficiency with modern containerization and orchestration tools. By building static binaries, containerizing your application, and leveraging managed services or serverless platforms, you can achieve rapid deployments and seamless scalability. Incorporating CI/CD pipelines, robust monitoring, and automated scaling ensures that your Go application not only performs well but also remains resilient and maintainable as demand grows.

12.2 Using Docker and Kubernetes with Go

Using Docker and Kubernetes with Go is a powerful approach to building, deploying, and scaling cloud-native applications. Go's ability to compile into static binaries makes it an ideal candidate for containerization, and Kubernetes provides a robust orchestration platform to manage and scale these containers efficiently.

1. Containerizing Go Applications with Docker
Static Binaries:

Go applications compile to single, self-contained binaries. This simplifies containerization since you don't need to include a complex runtime environment in your Docker image.

Dockerfile for Go:

A typical Dockerfile for a Go application uses multi-stage builds to reduce image size. For example:

Dockerfile
Copy code
```
# Build stage
FROM golang:1.19 AS builder
WORKDIR /app
COPY . .
RUN go mod download
```

```
RUN  CGO_ENABLED=0  GOOS=linux  go  build  -a
-installsuffix cgo -o myapp .

# Run stage
FROM alpine:latest
WORKDIR /app
COPY --from=builder /app/myapp .
ENTRYPOINT ["./myapp"]
```

This Dockerfile compiles your Go application in a Golang container and then copies the binary into a lightweight Alpine Linux image.

Benefits:

Portability: Containers encapsulate all dependencies, ensuring consistent environments across development, testing, and production.
Efficiency: Small image sizes and fast startup times improve deployment speed and resource utilization.

2. Orchestrating Go Applications with Kubernetes

Deployment Management:

Kubernetes manages containerized applications by defining deployments, which specify the desired state for your Go application pods. A typical deployment YAML file for a Go app might look like:

```yaml
yaml
Copy code
apiVersion: apps/v1
kind: Deployment
metadata:
  name: myapp-deployment
spec:
  replicas: 3
  selector:
    matchLabels:
      app: myapp
  template:
    metadata:
      labels:
        app: myapp
    spec:
      containers:
      - name: myapp
        image: your-docker-repo/myapp:latest
        ports:
```

```yaml
        - containerPort: 8080
```

This configuration deploys three replicas of your Go application, ensuring high availability and load balancing across pods.

Service Exposure:

To expose your deployment, you create a Kubernetes Service:

```yaml
yaml
Copy code
apiVersion: v1
kind: Service
metadata:
  name: myapp-service
spec:
  type: LoadBalancer
  selector:
    app: myapp
  ports:
  - port: 80
    targetPort: 8080
```

This service routes external traffic to your Go application pods, allowing seamless access and scaling.

Scaling and Health Checks:

Kubernetes supports horizontal pod autoscaling, which dynamically adjusts the number of replicas based on metrics like CPU utilization. Additionally, you can configure liveness and readiness probes in your pod specifications to monitor and ensure that your application is running correctly.

3. Integration and Best Practices

CI/CD Pipelines:

Integrate Docker builds and Kubernetes deployments into your CI/CD pipeline using tools like GitHub Actions, Jenkins, or GitLab CI. Automating tests, builds, and deployments ensures rapid and reliable delivery of updates.

Configuration Management:

Use Kubernetes ConfigMaps and Secrets to manage environment-specific configurations and sensitive information, keeping your container images generic and portable.

Monitoring and Logging:

Leverage Kubernetes-native tools like Prometheus, Grafana, and Fluentd to monitor performance, collect metrics, and aggregate logs. These insights are crucial for diagnosing issues and ensuring your Go application scales smoothly.

Conclusion

Combining Docker and Kubernetes with Go enables you to build, deploy, and scale cloud-native applications efficiently. Docker simplifies packaging by leveraging Go's static binaries, while Kubernetes provides powerful orchestration, scaling, and management features. Together, these tools facilitate rapid deployment, reliable performance, and robust scalability, making them an excellent choice for modern application development and operations.

12.3 Serverless Go with AWS Lambda and Google Cloud Functions

Serverless computing allows you to run your code without managing any underlying servers, and Go is a popular language choice in this paradigm due to its fast startup times, low memory footprint, and efficient performance. Both AWS Lambda and Google Cloud Functions support Go, enabling developers to build scalable, event-driven applications with minimal operational overhead.

AWS Lambda with Go

Overview:

AWS Lambda lets you run Go functions in response to various triggers such as API Gateway events, S3 uploads, or scheduled CloudWatch events. It automatically scales based on demand and you only pay for the compute time your code actually uses.

Developing a Lambda Function:

When writing a Lambda function in Go, you use the AWS Lambda Go SDK. Your function should have a handler signature that takes a context and an event, and then returns a response and an error. For example:

```go
Copy code
package main

import (
    "context"
    "fmt"

    "github.com/aws/aws-lambda-go/lambda"
)

// Handler is your Lambda function handler.
func Handler(ctx context.Context, event map[string]interface{}) (string, error) {
    // Process the event data.
    return fmt.Sprintf("Processed event: %v", event), nil
}

func main() {
    lambda.Start(Handler)
```

}This function can be triggered by various AWS services, processing incoming events and returning a response.

Deployment:

To deploy, compile your Go code for Linux:

bash
Copy code
GOOS=linux GOARCH=amd64 go build -o main
Package the binary into a ZIP file and upload it via the AWS Management Console, AWS CLI, or using frameworks like AWS SAM. AWS Lambda handles scaling and execution based on incoming events.

Google Cloud Functions with Go

Overview:

Google Cloud Functions supports Go for building lightweight, event-driven functions that respond to HTTP requests, Pub/Sub messages, or Cloud Storage events. Like AWS Lambda, it abstracts away server management and scales automatically with demand.

Developing a Cloud Function:

For an HTTP-triggered function in Google Cloud Functions, export a function that conforms to the required signature. For instance:

```go
Copy code
package function

import (
    "fmt"
    "net/http"
)

// HelloWorld is an HTTP Cloud Function.
func HelloWorld(w http.ResponseWriter, r *http.Request) {
    fmt.Fprintln(w, "Hello from Google Cloud Functions!")
}
```

This function is invoked when an HTTP request is made to its endpoint.

Deployment:Deploy the function using the gcloud CLI:

bash

Copy code

```
gcloud functions deploy HelloWorld --runtime go119
--trigger-http --allow-unauthenticated
```

Google Cloud Functions packages and deploys your code automatically, making it accessible via a public URL.

Best Practices for Serverless Go Applications

Optimize Cold Starts:

Even though Go functions compile to fast-starting binaries, reduce initialization overhead in your code to further minimize cold start delays.

Stateless Design:

Ensure your functions are stateless so that they can scale effortlessly. Any persistent state should be managed through external services like databases or caches.

Error Handling and Logging:

Handle errors gracefully and log meaningful messages. Use context to manage timeouts and cancellation, ensuring that functions do not run longer than necessary.

Monitoring and Observability:

Leverage cloud provider tools (AWS CloudWatch for Lambda, Google Cloud Logging and Monitoring for Cloud Functions) to monitor function performance, track invocations, and troubleshoot issues.

Security and Permissions:
Follow the principle of least privilege by assigning minimal necessary permissions to your functions. Use environment variables or secret management services to handle sensitive data securely.

Conclusion

Using Go in serverless environments like AWS Lambda and Google Cloud Functions offers a powerful, scalable, and cost-efficient way to build event-driven applications. Go's fast, compiled binaries and efficient resource usage complement the serverless model perfectly, allowing you to focus on your business logic while the cloud provider manages infrastructure, scaling, and availability. Whether you're processing API requests, handling data events, or building microservices, serverless Go enables rapid development and deployment with minimal overhead.

12.4 Monitoring and Logging in Production

Monitoring and logging in production are essential for ensuring the reliability, performance, and security of your applications. These practices help you understand system behavior, diagnose issues, and maintain operational efficiency in live environments.

Monitoring in Production

Purpose:

Monitoring collects metrics (like CPU usage, memory consumption, request latency, error rates, etc.) to provide a real-time view of your application's health and performance.

Instrumentation:

Integrate monitoring libraries (e.g., Prometheus client libraries) into your Go application to expose metrics endpoints. These endpoints can be scraped by monitoring systems to collect data over time.

```go
Copy code
import (
    "github.com/prometheus/client_golang/prometheus"

"github.com/prometheus/client_golang/prometheus/promhttp"
    "net/http"
)

var (
                        requestDuration    =
prometheus.NewHistogram(prometheus.HistogramOpts{
        Name: "http_request_duration_seconds",
        Help: "Duration of HTTP requests.",
    })
)
```

```go
func init() {
    prometheus.MustRegister(requestDuration)
}

func handler(w http.ResponseWriter, r *http.Request) {
    timer := prometheus.NewTimer(requestDuration)
    defer timer.ObserveDuration()
    w.Write([]byte("Hello, world!"))
}

func main() {
    http.Handle("/metrics", promhttp.Handler())
    http.HandleFunc("/", handler)
    http.ListenAndServe(":8080", nil)
}
```

Dashboards and Alerting:

Use tools like Grafana to visualize metrics collected by Prometheus. Set up alerts to notify you when critical thresholds are exceeded, ensuring proactive incident response.

Distributed Tracing:

For microservices, consider integrating distributed tracing systems (e.g., Jaeger, Zipkin) to trace requests across services. This helps identify latency bottlenecks and understand inter-service dependencies.

Logging in Production

Purpose:

Logging captures detailed information about application events, errors, and operational states. Logs are invaluable for troubleshooting, auditing, and understanding user behavior.

Structured Logging:

Use structured logging (e.g., JSON format) to output logs with key-value pairs. This makes it easier to search, filter, and analyze logs in log management systems.

```go
Copy code
import (
    "encoding/json"
    "log"
```

```go
    "os"
)

type LogEntry struct {
    Time    string `json:"time"`
    Level   string `json:"level"`
    Message string `json:"message"`
}

func main() {
    logger := log.New(os.Stdout, "", 0)
    entry := LogEntry{
        Time:    "2025-02-13T15:04:05Z",
        Level:   "INFO",
        Message: "Application started",
    }
    jsonEntry, _ := json.Marshal(entry)
    logger.Println(string(jsonEntry))
}
```

Centralized Log Management:

Aggregating logs from multiple instances into a centralized system (using tools like the ELK Stack, Splunk, or cloud-based logging solutions) allows you to correlate events across services and detect patterns that indicate issues.

Log Levels and Rotation:Implement log levels (e.g., DEBUG, INFO, WARN, ERROR) to control verbosity and ensure that critical issues are highlighted. Also, use log rotation and archival strategies to manage disk space and comply with data retention policies.

Best Practices

Correlate Metrics and Logs:

Combining monitoring metrics with logs provides a comprehensive picture of your application's behavior. Correlation helps pinpoint issues faster by connecting abnormal metrics with corresponding log entries.

Automate Alerting:

Set up automated alerts based on both metrics and logs to notify teams about anomalies, errors, or performance degradation.

Regularly Review and Update:

Continuously refine your monitoring and logging strategies based on operational experiences. Update dashboards, alert thresholds, and logging formats to adapt to changing requirements.

Security and Compliance:

Ensure that logs contain no sensitive information and are stored in compliance with relevant data protection standards. Secure access to both monitoring and logging systems to prevent unauthorized access.

Conclusion

Effective monitoring and logging in production are crucial for maintaining high availability, diagnosing issues, and ensuring optimal performance. By integrating robust instrumentation, using centralized systems for metrics and logs, and following best practices for alerting and data management, you can proactively manage your Go applications and respond swiftly to operational challenges.

www.ingramcontent.com/pod-product-compliance
Lightning Source LLC
LaVergne TN
LVHW022334060326
832902LV00022B/4036